Tales from
Michigan Stadium

Volume II

Jim Brandstatter

SP
SPORTS
PUBLISHING
L.L.C.

www.SportsPublishingLLC.com

ISBN: 1-58261-888-7

© 2005 by Jim Brandstatter

All photos except those otherwise indicated are courtesy of the University of Michigan Athletic Archives/Bob Kalmbach.

Publishers: Peter L. Bannon and Joseph J. Bannon Sr.
Senior managing editor: Susan M. Moyer
Acquisitions editor: Mike Pearson
Developmental editor: Elisa Bock Laird
Art director: K. Jeffrey Higgerson
Dust jacket design: Dustin Hubbart
Project manager: Jim Henehan
Imaging: Dustin Hubbart
Photo editor: Erin Linden-Levy
Vice president of sales and marketing: Kevin King
Media and promotions managers: Jonathan Patterson (regional),
    Randy Fouts (national), Maurey Williamson (print)

Printed in the United States of America

Sports Publishing L.L.C.
804 North Neil Street
Champaign, IL 61820

Phone: 1-877-424-2665
Fax: 217-363-2073
www.SportsPublishingLLC.com

Dedicated to
Arthur F. Brandstatter Sr.
1914–2004

Gone now, but never forgotten.
Thanks, Dad.

CONTENTS

PREFACE

If you are wondering who to blame for this second edition of *Tales from Michigan Stadium*, or *Tales from Michigan Stadium—Volume II* as we are calling this version, you needn't look any further than yourselves.

The Michigan football faithful were so very kind and generous in their acceptance of my first book that the publisher convinced me we needed to write another. We sold a lot more of the first book than anyone expected! The publisher was especially pleased once he recovered from the smelling salts. So the discussions about a second book started, and thank the Lord, here you are reading it, which means we've at least sold one copy.

Besides my deepest gratitude to all of you who bought and commented favorably on the first book, I must tell you I learned a lot in the process of writing that first group of tales.

One thing I learned rather quickly is not to make mistakes. If you make an error, I guarantee you will hear about it, and I did. I misidentified the hometown of one of the Michigan players in a story, and I got a letter about it. As a matter of fact, it was such a nice gentle correction that I'm going to use it as a tale for this book. The correction to my mistake appears on page 152. It deserves a full story, not just a paragraph in the preface.

Another thing I learned is that writing a book is like sharing a recipe. Everybody has a suggestion on how to make it better. I'm sure if any of you have shared a recipe, whomever you shared it with added a little something here or there, or they substituted a little something here or there. Well, in writing a book, you wonderful Wolverine fans were not shy at all in telling me that I didn't include anything about the marching band, and that I should be ashamed. I was.

It should also be noted that I was scolded, not harshly but good naturedly, because I never mentioned anything about the great tailgate society that has arisen over the years outside of

Michigan Stadium. There have been friendships forged for life thanks to a chance meeting in the parking lot of Pioneer High. Someone's front yard that happens to double as a parking lot on a Saturday afternoon in the fall has become the site of a yearly reunion. Parents watch their kids grow up at these tailgates. Now the kids are cooking the special tailgate recipes that have been passed down for generations as the parents sit in their lawn chairs, play with the grandkids, and reminisce about the great players and classic games during their days in Ann Arbor. So I will recount some tailgate-related tales, as I feel it is my duty to keep the tailgaters as happy as I can. It also will help me get free goodies as I walk through the Victors lot to my car after my postgame show.

Additionally I was told that I should include more stories about the modern-day teams and players. I agree with that, and I will include some tales about recent games and recent players. But I also feel obligated to include some of the older stories that I have been able to gather from some of the great Michigan men of the mid-1940s and 1950s and even before. To me, it is really important that we never forget the names of Yost, Crisler, Oosterbaan, and the like. They are the cornerstones of the Michigan tradition, and we need to keep their names alive.

Think about it. There are kids out there today who don't realize how important the 1969 Michigan victory over Ohio State was to this program. The biggest game in their memory may be the 1998 Rose Bowl that clinched a national title. That's a huge game, no question about it, but the history of Michigan football is the foundation that the 1998 national championship is built upon. Besides, I played in that 1969 Wolverine win over the Buckeyes, and I don't want anyone to forget that. And I don't want anyone, especially the younger fans, to miss the opportunity to get to know about a guy like Bo Schembechler, who was in his first season in 1969. To forget those guys is to forget why Michigan football stands above the rest.

So, those are the some of the reasons you are getting *Tales from Michigan Stadium—Volume II.* There are other reasons, too.

I did receive a number of very kind notes and letters from people who were moved by some of the stories in the first book. These notes and letters made me realize how much I had taken my association with Michigan for granted. I am so close to the program, and have been for so many years, that I think I had forgotten the emotional attachment other Wolverine fans have for Michigan, especially those who have moved to other states. They may only get one or two trips a year to The Big House, and they've got to squeeze everything they can into those trips. The first *Tales from Michigan Stadium* really impacted them, and in turn, they impacted me.

A letter from a guy named Richard Freeman, who lives in Georgia, convinced me another book was necessary. Freeman wrote the letter to Coach Schembechler and also sent a copy to me after he had read the first book. What follows is an excerpt from that letter that moved me enough to start working on *Volume II.*

Dear Coach Schembechler,

By way of background, I am from Ann Arbor. I was born there, and essentially raised on South State Street— very close to the Michigan Stadium. In fact, the house is still there. My father used to fly over the stadium while a photographer for the Ann Arbor News. *He took pictures of the game and the crowd. Yes, it goes back to just after World War II.*

As a kid I used to park cars in our front yard and in the driveway. Once we were full up, I would run out our back door, cut through the University of Michigan Golf Course, get into the stadium, and watch the Wolverines play football. While I ended up attending a different Big Ten school, the Maize and Blue runs very deep in me.

They are my team, pure and simple.

Even when I am reduced to watching them on TV, there is no sitting down… I pace the entire game in front of the TV and "coach" the heck out of the game, and assist the officials as well. Drives my wife nuts, too!

At the close of Jim's book, he makes reference to the walk from the practice field across the tracks to the Stadium. Well Coach Schembechler, I have made that walk many times—but of course, short of getting into the tunnel and down onto the field. Just sitting here writing this gives me goose bumps. It is hallowed ground.

There is nothing like Michigan Football and all that goes with it. Nothing. Jim's book captures the essence of what that tradition is all about.

Best Regards,
Dick Freeman

Hopefully *Tales from Michigan Stadium—Volume II* will have a similar impact on many of you. I hope you enjoy these tales as much as you did the first set.

ACKNOWLEDGMENTS

Special thanks to Mike DeBord, Scott Loeffler, Gary Moeller, Joe Donovan, Howard King, Jack Lane, Mike Lantry, J.D. Carlson, Monte Robbins, Vada Murray, John Mooney, Richard Freeman, Mike Kenn, Steve Everitt, Doug James, Rod Payne, Bill Dufek, Gordon Bell, Billy Taylor, Butch Woolfolk, Tom Goss, Grant Bowman, Bill Yearby, Tim Davis, Calvin O'Neal, Phil Seymour, Victor Hobson, Tom Stincic, Tom Hassel, Frank Nunley, Dan Cline, Ted Cachey, Dave Rentschler, Howard Wikel, Matt Pickus, Bo Schembechler, Carl Grapentine, Dennis Franklin, Michael Taylor, John Kolesar, Braylon Edwards, Craig Dunaway, Tai Streets, Mel Lester, Ira Jaffe, Dave Schultz, Ernest Shazor, Bruce Elliott, George Hoey, Jeff Cohen, Clare Canham-Eaton, Pat Perry, Andy Cannavino, Tom Seabron, and Bob Thornbladh.

Additional thanks to Robbie Brandstatter and Mary W. Brandstatter, proofreaders.

Finally—in memorium Don Canham and Dr. Gerry O'Connor.

CHAPTER ONE

Tailgates

The life behind the party

Tailgates are a big part of the Michigan Stadium experience. *Michigan Replay*, the coach's show that I co-host with coach Lloyd Carr, has always had a tailgate. We probably started it in the early to mid-1980s. Allen Sieger, who was a propmaster at WXYZ and had worked on the show since it started in 1970 at Channel 7 in Detroit, didn't want to give up his involvement after the program went independent, so he was made our official tailgate party guy. He took it seriously. I mean, this guy has a subscription to *Bon Appetit* magazine. Needless to say, our tailgate took on a life of its own. We have graduated from paper plates to stainless steel chafing dishes. Sieger bought a Chevy

Suburban to haul the heater ovens, grills, tents, and serving trays from St. Clair Shores to Ann Arbor. We've had lobster, alligator, emu, beef tenderloin, Italian sausage (my favorite), and just about everything else that is exotic or edible. Our executive producer, Bob Lipson, even gave Sieger a credit on the screen at the end of the show. How many times have you seen a coach's show with TV credits that list a tailgate coordinator with the associate producer?

Your friendly neighborhood tailgate

There are two guys from the East Coast who were transplanted to the Midwest, and they always have clam chowder or lobster for me. They also partake of an occasional adult beverage, I think, and sound a lot like Norm and Cliff on *Cheers*.

It's not just for the fans

John Wangler's mom always has a huge tailgate. You can walk by that one and get some pretty good autographs of former players on most Saturdays. I remember when the late Leo Calhoun used to bring his motor home into the lot, park it just outside the entrance of Crisler Arena, and feed hundreds. Calhoun's paint job on the motor home was a work of art. There were hand-painted action scenes of Ron Kramer and other Michigan greats adorning the length of the RV.

Tent-gating in style

One of the most amazing tailgates is just outside the Stadium tunnel entrance on a grassy hill above the driveway between the two parking areas. It is the tailgate of Mel Lester and Ira Jaffe. Calling it a tailgate is a misnomer, because there isn't a car with a tailgate near it. It is a party under a tent!

"We are in our 31st year tailgating together," Dr. Lester says proudly. "Before we joined forces, we were tailgating separately but right next to each other. We didn't even know each other. We met at an event that had nothing to do with Michigan football. We discovered we were tailgating next to each other and put our tailgates together."

It is still going strong, and when I say strong, it is an understatement.

"We usually have 20 dozen donuts," Jaffe says matter-of-factly. "We have 50 dozen bagels. I would say 20 to 30 pounds of corned beef, tuna, roast beef, turkey, salami, and I could keep on going. We pay for all of it ourselves.

"We invite the community, but I'm not sure what that means. Everybody comes by; some of the guards come by early; we have friends stop by. We have students who will see us somewhere other than the tailgate, and they'll say, 'You don't know me, Dr. Lester or Mr. Jaffe, but you fed me for four years."

And whomever they feed gets a treat each game.

"I change the menu every week," Lester says with a smile. "We never do the same thing twice. My daughter, Stephanie, is the chili expert, so we will do 15 gallons of chili along with pasta dishes, beef tenderloin sandwiches, salads, and all kinds of things.

"We probably feed six or seven hundred for each game now, but I don't care. When we got to 300, I quit counting, and now I don't even bother."

I was born Blue

It all started, innocently enough, 25 years ago when Dave Schultz was invited to a Wolverine game and tailgate party by a manager he knew from a Ford plant.

"I knew they had a lot of great food at the tailgate," Schultz says as the grill sizzles. "Well, I wanted to bring something to the party that was unique to the area I grew up [in Pinconning, Michigan], so when I came down for that first tailgate, I brought a dozen filets of perch with a single burner Coleman stove. Now, 25 years later, I'm up to 2,000 filets at the last home game every year."

Now, understand, Schultz did not graduate from Michigan. He is like so many others who have family or friends who have a Michigan affiliation, and they just fall in love with the entire program. In Schultz's case, it's a family affair.

"More than half of our family are Michigan graduates," he says with pride. "In fact, we just celebrated my dad's 50th anniversary of his graduation from pharmacy school. So don't worry, I was born Blue!"

One of the keys to cooking perch is the batter or breading that is used. There are thousands of homemade beer batters and the like. These recipes can be fiercely private secrets. To my surprise, Schultz was more than happy to pass his concoction along.

"The breading is 60 percent Kellogg's corn flakes, 40 percent flour," Schultz divulges. "The spices are a personal choice, whatever you or your friends like will do. The key, though, the grease has to be 350 to 375 degrees whether there is wind or no wind. Actually," Schultz laughs, "try and keep the wind at your back. Then cook each filet two to three minutes depending on its size. And always use peanut oil for your grease."

CHAPTER TWO

The Band

Making the band

If you think it is competitive to be on the Michigan football team, you should see what it takes to make the cut for the marching band that performs on Saturdays. You've got to be good. You've got to be tough. You've got to get a break at times. And most importantly, you've got to be incredibly dedicated to achieving the goal. It is an accomplishment that should make anyone proud.

"There are actually about 400 people in the band," former drum major Matt Pickus explains, "but you only see 250 at half-time. The 250 that you see is called the *performance block*. The rest of the group is called the *reserves*. It keeps everybody on their toes, because the people in the performance block want to stay there, and the reserves want to move up. And there is competition for spots in the performance block every week."

Although this competitive atmosphere may sound a bit like a pressure cooker, it certainly creates the environment to bring out the best in people. It also ensures that on Saturday you are getting the absolute best 250 performers that the band has to offer. But two weeks before the season begins, it is even more demanding, because the members go through band week, a grueling time similar to the physical and mental stress of two-a-days.

"During band week," Pickus says, "everybody looks at everybody else. The entire band actually votes on who makes the performance block and who doesn't. One rank at a time of 12 members marches in front of the marching band playing 'The Victors,' and the entire band votes on who did better or who did worse. Everyone's heads are down and their eyes are closed, so it is a private vote. That's how the performance block is set for the first game. It is by a vote of the band."

Talk about high drama. Yet these band members are willing to go through it for the opportunity to go out on the floor of Michigan Stadium every Saturday wearing their own Maize and Blue uniforms.

Majoring in band

The audition process is nothing compared to what candidates for drum major go through.

"The first thing I should tell you," Pickus says with pride, "is that I was in the marching band for seven years. I am particular about one point. I got my undergraduate degree in four years and went immediately into grad school so I could stay in the band.

"Anyway, on the third day of band week are the drum major tryouts. The band votes by written ballot on the drum major. They don't vote until the candidates complete a 10-event tryout. It is like a decathlon!"

The one-day audition starts off with an interview by the entire band where the candidate has to answer two questions: What is a Michigan drum major? and Why would you make a good drum major? After the verbal drilling comes the marching and command tests. The potential drum major strikes the position of attention, turns to the side to give the band a profile view, and marches down the field. The people in the band judge the person on vocal and whistle commands and the goalpost toss. While carrying out whistle commands and with only a drummer behind you, the candidate marches 20 yards in low stride. Then he or she follows the same protocol to the tune of "The Victors," which is a 40-yard march. Next comes the "optional" baton twirling contest, which almost all candidates do. Then the contenders showcase their entrances, which consists of a run on the field, a right turn, a high kick, and a backbend. Finally the last test is The Strut, where the person leans way back and high kicks.

After all 400 pairs of eyes have watched their every move, the votes are cast and tallied. The drum major is announced that night.

Pickus went through it three times before he was rewarded with victory, and he was so good that in his last year in the band, he was the only candidate to try out for drum major. But even though he was the only one, he still had to complete all 10 events and the band still had to vote.

Backing it up

The backbend that seems to have become almost a prerequisite for the drum major began in 1971 when Mark Brown leaned back and touched the plume of his hat to the ground between his heels. Every drum major after that has had their own bent on how to do it.

"Nobody really teaches you how to do these things," former drum major Matt Pickus explains. "You work with past drum majors or other marching band members. When I tried out for the drum major position, I worked with every drum major from

1971 on until I got the job. I talked to Mark Brown. I talked with the guy who did backflips instead of the backbend. I even went back to the drum major from 1950, Dick Smith, and worked with him. He was the drum major for Michigan when *Life* magazine put him on the cover. It was when I was working with past drum major Ian Stines that I realized how close I was on the backbend."

Stines was helping Pickus practice for his first drum major tryout when Pickus decided to try the backbend. As he came up, Stines stared at him with eyes as big as saucers.

"You came about this far from touching your head!" Stines exclaimed amazed as he held his hands about 12 inches apart.

"You're kidding!" Pickus responded.

He wondered if he could do it and get back up, and even if he could, he wasn't sure he could make it look good. He kept trying to perfect it for the big day.

The day came, and during the entrance test, Pickus bent back, touched his head to the ground at Elbel Field, and came back up. The whole band erupted in cheers.

"The whole band went crazy!" Pickus remembers. "I still lost the competition for drum major."

Three attempts later, Pickus won and became the drum major.

"A week after I won, the first football game was scheduled," he remembers. "Well, I spent that entire week working with the band, because the drum major's responsibility is to get the band onto the field so that they perform to the utmost of their potential. Everything else that you do is secondary. So I was concentrating on the band, and everything was brand new to me. We had rehearsals in the Stadium. It was 12-hour days during band week.

"We marched to the Stadium, and that was wonderful," Pickus remembers with a smile, "we got into the tunnel and everything is just great, and it's fun. We sing 'The Yellow and the Blue,' and then the teams go through, and we squish up against the side of the tunnel when the opponents come by and we don't say a word. We look straight ahead. It is dead silent."

Then one of the marching band staff looked straight at Pickus.

"Matt, bring 'em down!" he yelled.

The band ran out the tunnel and stood behind their fearless leader. Pickus turned around, looked right at the snare drummer, and waited for band announcer Carl Grapentine's deep voice to call them into action. The magical words called Pickus to action.

"Baaaaaand, take the field!"

Pickus started the cadence and blew the whistle. The band ran out onto the field exactly the way they should. They struck up the "M Fanfare"—and that was when it hit Pickus: "I am the Michigan drum major! What in the hell have I done?"

Despite the five years he had spent in the band and all of the failed tryouts he had gone through, the fear hit him hard.

"Don't run back into the tunnel!" he told himself as he prepared for his signature moment.

Before the game it had been decided that Pickus would leave his hat on for the backbend.

"When I bent over backward, the hat was heavy," Pickus remembers. "I had been used to seeing the ground about three yards away from me because I had been practicing without the hat. With the hat on and the brim in the way of my eyes, the ground was maybe 30 yards away. And I lost my balance. So I stood up and I got set, went over backward, and forgot about the plume, I smacked the top of the hat to the ground and got back up, and I went on my way."

That was the only game for which he wore the hat.

The next time Pickus had the chance to perform his unique hatless backbend in front of the Michigan Stadium crowd was the next home game against Notre Dame. Pickus had extra incentive to unveil his masterpiece this time, because before the game, a fan had come up to him and poked him in the chest.

"So, how many times is it going to take you to do the backbend today?" he sniped.

Pickus was astonished at the brashness but didn't miss a beat.

The amazing Matt Pickus performs his unique signature back-bend. *Courtesy of Matt Pickus*

"Sir, when you watch pregame today," he responded, "you will see something that has never ever been done before in Michigan Stadium."

The confrontation set the tone for a momentous pregame band show.

"I was really too nervous to pay much attention to the crowd," Pickus recalls. "I remember going out there, and everything was perfect. The 'M Fanfare' is being played, I'm following the twirlers. I take the corner, and I do the high kick. Then I stop and take the hat *off* and put it on my hip. I bend over backwards, and I touch the ground. I go all the way down to my head. I stand up, flourish to the crowd, and go on my way.

"The guy that I first worked with on the backbend, Ian Stines, came over to me and asked, 'What in the hell happened during pregame?' Ian had been playing in the trombone section on the other side of the field, and he couldn't see me. I said, 'Why?' I had no idea what he was talking about. He said, 'Because all of a sudden the crowd got quieter than I've ever heard them and then louder than it's ever been.' I still had no idea what he meant."

It wasn't until they looked at a tape of the backbend that it all made sense. The crowd got quiet when Pickus took the hat off and put it on his hip.

"They didn't have a clue what I was doing with the hat," Pickus recalls. "They thought I was going to touch the plume to the ground. When I took it off, they were surprised. Then, when I started the backbend, you could hear a murmuring on the tape. It's almost as if they were saying, 'What's he doing?' It got quieter and quieter the closer I got to the ground. And when I smacked my head to the ground and came back up, it got loud. It was incredibly loud. That was my first hatless backbend!"

He never did another backbend wearing a hat, and the tradition he started carries on today.

As a side note, the rude fan who chastised Pickus after his first off-balance backbend did come back and apologize two weeks later. Pickus was standing at attention in front of the band just outside the tunnel when he felt another poke in his ribs, looked over, and saw the same fan.

"I couldn't react because I was at attention," Pickus remembers, "but the guy said, 'I know you're working right now and can't really say anything or move, but I just want to tell you I'm really sorry. That move you made the last game was the most incredible thing I've ever seen.' And he walked away. To this day, I still have no idea who the guy was."

The absolute first visitor

William D. Revelli began his career at Michigan as the director of the University of Michigan bands in 1935. He was the fourth major name to direct the bands program since 1906, when Eugene Fischer was accepted to be the first individual to run them. In 1915, Wilfred Wilson followed Fischer, and Wilson was succeeded by Nicholas Falcone in 1927. The longest run at the helm of the bands program amongst these three men was 12 years by Wilson from 1915 to 1926. When Revelli took over in 1935, he did not relinquish control of the program until 1972. It was an incredible 38-year era of growth and excellence in the Michigan bands. It is said that when Revelli took over, he breathed new life into the program. He invigorated the students he inherited, and he recruited new students like a football coach.

It is interesting that Revelli was compared to a football coach at times. He was a disciple of discipline. He was tough on those who played and marched for him. He demanded excellence. In a paper entitled "The Five Requisites of a Successful Musical Performance," Revelli even sounds like a football coach:

> *Good tone quality is the result of correct fundamental preparation and requires the correct mental, auditory conception of beauty and tone; plus the ability to perceive the color, quality and image of the tone to be produced.*
>
> *It is amazing how effectively this phase of the students' development can be realized; yet it remains perhaps the most deficient of the five essential elements of performance.*

There is no question that Revelli got results. His bands from the very beginning had an edge on all of the others. He already had a national reputation in the early 1930s. That reputation of excellence stayed with him until the day he retired from Michigan, and he made sure that it carried over into other departments as well.

In 1969 when Bo Schembechler was named the head football coach at Michigan, it didn't take long for him to learn and like the man who led the bands.

"I came to Michigan in nineteen hundred and sixty nine," Schembechler says in his best staccato delivery. "I'm in my office, and the first visitor that I get, *the absolute first visitor,*" Schembechler pauses for dramatic effect, then lowers his voice, "is William D. Revelli."

That day in 1969 Revelli sat down in the coach's office and paused.

"I want you to know that I coach my band exactly the same way you coach your football team. We'll have discipline, and we'll do it the way it's supposed to be done!"

William Revelli leads the band in his last performance at Michigan Stadium. *Courtesy of Matt Pickus*

The coach was impressed as he listened to the man continue his speech about excellence.

"We must have talked for a half an hour," Coach Schembechler recalls years later. "We got to know each other, and I liked him right away.

"As a coach, I had never operated with a band of that caliber. It was a precision machine that sounded great, too. I can remember when we came in early in the fall for practice, so did the band. So I'd invite Bill over with the band to play after practice, and he'd bring 'em over."

The relationship between the two grew, and Coach Schembechler's love of Revelli's passion for Michigan prompted the coach to come up with a plan to use Revelli as his team's musical coach.

"I asked Bill over to the football meeting rooms early in the fall during our first practices," the former coach remembers with a smile, "and I asked him to teach the incoming freshman players how to sing 'The Victors.' He was absolutely great with the kids. He told them how this great fight song was written."

Schembechler lowers his voice to a near whisper.

"He said John Phillip Souza called this the greatest fight song *ever!* He went on to tell the kids about the great players of the past who had played at Michigan. He regaled them about some of the great games of the past. Oh, he knew football. He followed football."

Revelli then looked at the entire group of young freshman football players gathered around after he had given them his history lesson.

"Now, we're going to learn to sing 'The Victors!'" he said.

Revelli brought out his pitch pipe and began the official instructions.

"You sing from down in here, in your diaphragm," Revelli lectured. "You bring it up from down there with feeling."

Then he blew the starting note on his pitch pipe.

"Let's go!" he shouted.

"Hail to the Victors, valiant—" the students began to sing.

"No, No, No!" he yelled. "That's terrible! There's no enthusiasm. You don't sing it without enthusiasm!"

So the freshmen started again, and they got a little further into the song and then—

"No, no, no!"

And then again. A wrong note.

"No, no, no!" Revelli shouted. "We're gonna get this right if I'm here all night!"

A half hour later the freshmen were able to hit every note with the appropriate amount of gusto.

"He was absolutely great," Coach Schembechler muses as he shakes his head, "and the freshmen absolutely loved it. And let me tell you, every one of those freshmen came out of that session with Revelli knowing 'The Victors.' They knew the *words,* they knew how to *sing it,* and they knew how to *emphasize* the right spots. They flat out knew *how to do it.* And it was only because he came over there with the idea that those guys were going to come out of that meeting room knowing how to sing this fight song the right way or else! And they did. That was Bill Revelli."

Revelli died in 1994 at age 92. His name remains in history books as one of the great music educators of the past century. There are a great many young men who had learned "The Victors" from Revelli who would, no doubt, agree.

"You know, I spoke at his funeral," Coach Schembechler recalls, "and I told that story about Bill teaching the freshmen how to sing 'The Victors.' I wanted the people to know what he was like. How he was so connected to football. I don't think there is a bandsman out there now who is connected to football like he was. And he *knew* football."

He was just reaming people out

Director of bands William Revelli was known for his high standards when it came to performance, and he used some interesting tactics to get the results he wanted. One afternoon in 1971, the marching band was rehearsing as they did for every game, but this time the practice was not going as he had envisioned. He screamed at the band and picked out individuals in it who, according to him, weren't doing their jobs correctly.

Finally he turned to the entire band in disgust.

"Just march up and down the field!" he shouted.

The band members were standing around Revelli and were very quiet. They turned to begin their punishment: They marched up and down the field, up and down the field.

Standing about six inches from the livid genius was the brand new voice of the marching bands, Carl Grapentine, who didn't really know what to do. He looked at the ground, not wanting to make eye contact with the angered man as the band continued to march.

Tap! Tap!

Someone touched Grapentine's shoulder, and so he turned, only to come face to face with the man who had just reamed everyone out.

"Oh God, maybe I'm supposed to go down on the field and march!" he thought to himself.

"Yes sir?" he asked timidly and looked down.

Revelli was holding his wallet. He thrust a piece of paper toward his awaiting victim.

"Here's a picture of some fish I caught in Canada this summer."

Grapentine was surprised as he looked at the director's catch.

"It made me wonder how much of his persona was an act sometimes," Grapentine proposes after laughing at the memory. "He had the band down there sweating like crazy and getting yelled at, and I was up with him looking at fishing pictures."

Double duty

After 35 years as the marching band announcer, Carl Grapentine has managed to balance his job as the band's announcer with his real day job. Grapentine is currently the morning rush hour host on Chicago's classical radio station WFMT. Before his 19 years in Chicago, he worked in Detroit on a classical radio station. His commitment to Michigan and the band is remarkable. He has seen nine different conductors come and go and has read countless halftime and pregame scripts. In the time he has been the voice of the band, he has only missed two games, which came this past season when he had some medical issues he needed to address. But the band didn't have to adjust much. Grapentine's younger brother, Chris, filled in for him. Chris Grapentine is a band alumnus, and Grapentine says they sound a lot alike, so it was as if nobody knew he had been gone.

That may not have been the case back in 1975, when Grapentine had to pull double duty at Michigan Stadium— even if it was for only one play. Howard King, the Michigan Stadium PA announcer, does not sound like Grapentine, but that didn't stop Grapentine from stepping in when King was not at his post.

"In his 33 years as the PA man, Howard has missed one play," Grapentine recalls with a smile. "It was the 1975 Northwestern game. We won the game 69-0, I think. Well, after halftime, Howard wasn't around. They are lining up for the kickoff, and there is no Howard! I'm in the announcer booth, and we're looking around, and someone said, 'I guess you better do it,' and pointed at me!

"Since it was a shutout, this kickoff was going to be the only play of the entire game that the Northwestern kicker was in for. Well, I looked down to get the kicker's name and announce it. It had to be seven syllables long! So I had to say, 'Kicking off for Northwestern, number whatever,' and then try to get this kid's name right."

Grapentine did the job as well as he could, and King arrived back for the next play, having been delayed because of a crowded press box restroom. But Grapentine likes to kid King about the "real" reason he was late.

"Howard didn't want to say that kicker's name," Grapentine jokes.

(By the way, the kicker was a young freshman named Nick Mirkopulos who handled their placement duties and still holds the Wildcats' record with a 54-yarder against Arizona.)

Soundproof boxes

A t the end of the 1975 season, the Michigan football squad was tapped as the first team in Big Ten history to go to a bowl game other than the Rose Bowl. They were selected to play Oklahoma in the Orange Bowl. Because the situation was unique, NBC loved the matchup—Oklahoma versus Michigan, two traditional powers battling on New Year's night. In a nutshell, the game was huge. In a game like this, the Michigan Marching Band was a sure bet to be there. And if the band was there, band announcer Carl Grapentine would be there, too.

The announcer booth at the Orange Bowl press box was different from most booths Grapentine had worked. It was enclosed, and it was almost soundproof. He also had to be hooked up to this contraption that included a headset with heavy ear covers. The headset made it nearly impossible to hear much of the ambient sound in the stadium below. The crowd noise was effectively eliminated for the public address announcer. In order to speak, Grapentine also had to press a button on a cable attached to more equipment and amplifiers. It was this situation that created one of Grapentine's most memorable moments as a PA man.

During the pregame for the Orange Bowl, Grapentine, the fans, and the TV crews were waiting for the Rose Bowl, which was being broadcast by NBC, to end so that NBC's coverage of the Orange Bowl could begin. The Rose Bowl battle between Ohio State, which was favored to win the national championship, and UCLA was running late when UCLA scored to put the game away and end the Buckeyes' hopes of the title.

Suddenly the door to the announcer booth opened, and a man rushed in frantically.

"We've got to announce the Rose Bowl score!" he yelled. "The fans here don't know."

One of the Orange Bowl technicians turned to the guy.

"I've got the Michigan band announcer hooked up already," he said, pointing at Grapentine.

They both stared at the band announcer.

"I'll do it," Grapentine replied without any hesitation.

He put on his headset and pushed the little button to activate the mic.

"Fourth-quarter score from the Rose Bowl in Pasadena, UCLA 23, Ohio State 10," he said, waiting for the expected roar from the crowd.

Nothing. Silence.

"That's weird," he thought, knowing that the Michigan fans love to see their rival lose, and the Oklahoma crowds should have been going crazy because the Buckeyes were ahead of them in the rankings. Grapentine figured that the thick headset and the soundproof booth just muffled the noise.

As it turned out, that wasn't exactly the case.

"As I'm walking on the field in front of the band seats, they're yelling at me, 'Hey Grape, way to go, way to go.' Well, it turns out," Grapentine explains, "when I gave the score of the Ohio State game, Oklahoma quarterback Steve Davis was giving the invocation prayer, and right in the middle of that prayer my voice comes booming through, 'Fourth-quarter score from Pasadena...'

"I didn't even know that I had done it. They even mentioned it in *Sports Illustrated* the next week. They called me an overzealous PA announcer."

You're the biggest bad ass to ever walk in here

Rivalries bring out the best in people, and for Michigan fans, there are no greater opponents than Ohio State and Michigan State. Any chance we can get to tweak them—especially in their home stadiums—is worth it.

One time at the hallowed Horseshoe, two-season drum major Matt Pickus was the instrument of just such a snubbing. As he led the band out on the field at Ohio Stadium, band announcer Carl Grapentine was ready to add a little jab to the ritual pregame.

"And now, ladies and gentlemen, Michigan's man upfront, from Shaker Heights, Ohio—Matt Pickus!"

The boos were deafening.

But that wasn't the only impression Pickus made on the Buckeye faithful. The summer before his last year as drum major, Pickus interned in Columbus and used Ohio State's band practice fields to work out. Because he was an Ohio native, he was well aware of the animosity that the rabid Buckeye faithful felt for the true-blue Wolverine. But Pickus grew up a Wolverine and his parents were staunch Wolverines, so nothing was going to change their Maize and Blue blood. He planned to make that clear that season when Michigan played Ohio State in the Horseshoe.

When game day approached, Pickus was focused and ready to go. The band had gathered across the street from Ohio Stadium where they had to march through the primarily scarlet and gray crowds to the tunnel entrance. The members huddled together tightly so that the Buckeye fans would not infiltrate their ranks and cause trouble as had happened in the past. They literally walked heel to toe and shoulder to shoulder. Pickus was in front as their leader, and he followed an Ohio state trooper who escorted the band through the gathered masses to the stadium's tunnel.

Because Pickus wanted to display an air of toughness in this hostile setting, he didn't smile or react to any comment. His eyes stayed forward. His shoulders were back. His posture was like a military man at attention. As they proceeded across the streets to the stadium, the state trooper kept giving Pickus verbal directions. Pickus nodded at him imperceptibly and moved the long column in the proper direction. After a while, the trooper stopped talking and just pointed at the turns. Pickus never reacted; he just got the column moving in the right direction.

After they reached the tunnel entrance and were preparing for their march into the stadium, the state trooper moved so he was standing right next to Pickus.

"You're probably the biggest bad ass I've ever seen walk in here," the cop mentioned quietly.

He left, and Pickus couldn't help but smile.

"I thought it was one of the biggest compliments I've ever gotten," Pickus remembers.

Last-minute adjustments

At the same Michigan–Ohio State game, the Michigan band had been asked to shorten and amend their pregame show, because Ohio State had a pregame ceremony scheduled. In this particular instance, it meant the band could only use half of the field instead of the whole field for their "M Fanfare" and that the middle of the "V" of the block "M" would be at the 10-yard line instead of the 50. Everyone would have to adjust. That included the drum major, Matt Pickus.

"Because I was from Ohio, I really understood the rivalry," Pickus says. "I was a veteran, and I knew how loud Ohio Stadium could get, so I spent a lot of time warning the band. I kept telling them this was going to be different. I told them they had to pay attention visually, because they weren't going to be able to hear.

"All the while I was warning the band to be focused and watch closely, I was trying to figure out what I had to do. I had to run out to the middle of the 'V' in the block 'M' and turn left instead of right. Then I had to figure how far down the field I had to run before performing the high kick and backbend. At home in Michigan Stadium, I went from the 50 to the 20. That was 30 yards. Since I was starting on the 10 at Ohio Stadium, that meant I ran to the 40. Well, because the band was compressed at one end of the field, the flag carriers were going to be at the same end of the formation as the twirlers. I usually went five yards past the last outside group to do my backbend. As I was pondering this, I was adding the numbers and I thought, 'If I'm going to go all the way out to the 45-yard line, why don't I just make it the 50?'

Matt Pickus's last-minute change to his routine led to this career-highlight at Ohio State. *Courtesy of Matt Pickus*

"I practiced it that way all week long. On that game day, as soon as we get announced by Carl, the boos started. We couldn't even hear Carl finish the introduction. I blow my whistle, and we take the field. The crowd is booing like crazy. We get in position, and Carl announces the 'M Fanfare,' and you literally cannot hear anything. The conductor is waving his arms, but you can't hear anything, because the crowd is so loud. When it came time for the drum major introduction, I am running through 235 people blowing their faces off, and I can't hear them!

"It is also the only time I ever smiled on the field. My mother always used to get mad at me because all the pictures I had as the drum major were so serious. I was very militaristic when I was in front of that band. I never smiled. But on this day, running through that band with all those people booing, I was laughing. I had a grin from ear to ear!

"When I got to the 50-yard line, I did my high kick, and the crowd went dead silent! Then, I bent over and touched my head to the ground on the backbend. I got back up and dropped into the splits while holding my arms up over my head in a salute that I do, and the crowd started booing again but louder than before. *I had done all this right in the middle of the block 'O' at Ohio Stadium!"*

(Pickus never intended this as an insult to Ohio State. It just happened that with the change in positioning on the field because of the shortened pregame, which was scheduled by Ohio State, his routine came at the 50-yard line. It was a matter of following a procedure and plan that was in place long before the Ohio State game came up on the schedule. If the pregame had been normal, Pickus would have been at the 20 when all this happened. There was no disrespect to Ohio State intended.)

"My resumé states to this day that I was elected two years in a row as the drum major of the Michigan Marching Band," Pickus chuckles, "and just below that I have printed, 'Frequently cheered by over 100,000 people, and once, personally booed by 90,000 people!'"

With a resumé like that, I'll hire you—anytime.

CHAPTER THREE

The Voices

The voice of Michigan Stadium

There are those who suggest that I am the voice of Michigan football. I appreciate and am humbled by these compliments, but I respectfully disagree. There are many voices of Michigan football. You could make a case for my partner on WJR radio broadcasts, Frank Beckmann. You could make a case for Tom Hemingway, who broadcast the Wolverines for years on WUOM. The point is that down through the years there have been many voices, and all of them have done outstanding work.

In my opinion, though, there was really only one voice of Michigan football, and that was Bob Ufer. When Ufer passed away, he took the title of the voice with him. It should stay with Ufer forever.

Now the voice of Michigan Stadium is another person. For more than 32 years, it has been Howard King. You've heard him every game in The Big House since the early 1970s. King is the public address announcer at the Stadium. The job has been a labor of love for King ever since he started in 1973. He retired from his regular job back in 1998 and moved with his wife, Liz, to Traverse City, but that didn't stop him from his duties at Michigan Stadium.

Over the years, King admits the job has changed dramatically.

"To get ready for games now, I drive down early Friday morning," King says, "That's one of the changes that happened over the last 30 years, I used to amble into the press box a couple of hours before the game, do the game, then go home, and have dinner. It doesn't happen that way anymore.

"I now have meetings on Fridays around noon with people from athletics. I will go over to the sports information department and do some homework for the next day's game."

It is clearly a lot different than it was back in the early days, and King says the reason is technology.

"Mainly," King explains, "I have to coordinate the Jumbotron screen on the scoreboard with the announcements I have.

"There are so many more announcements," King says, "There are many, many, more. I must have 22 or 23 pages of promotional announcements. There are no commercial announcements, of course; they are all promotional and informational regarding Michigan athletics."

If you've been to one game or if you've been to a hundred, there is one announcement that you always remember as you leave the Stadium at the conclusion of a game. We hear King intone the famous words that are reassuring to us all as we file out.

"Ann Arbor Police advise us that Ann Arbor-Saline Road will be one way to I-94 immediately after the game. Thank you."

Don't throw the snowballs

One of the more interesting moments in the press box for Howard King during his years as the PA announcer came under the watchful and sometimes intimidating eye of athletic director Don Canham.

It was late in the season, and King was just finishing up calling the runner and tackler. All of a sudden a voice bellowed from right over his head.

"Tell 'em not to throw the snowballs!"

King finished what he was saying. He was annoyed at the interruption by the voice he couldn't put a name to. He turned around and came nose to nose with Canham.

"Tell 'em not to throw the snowballs!" he reiterated.

Now King was in a tough spot, so he said what he thought.

"Don, if we do that, it's going to make it worse, not better."

Canham glared at King,

"Tell 'em to stop throwing the damn snowballs!" he insisted.

King turned back to the microphone.

"Please, in consideration for others around you, stop throwing snowballs," he said softly and gently. "Someone might be injured if you continue throwing snowballs."

After the meek announcement, Canham stomped out of the booth—and never interrupted King again.

Slippery Rock

In Michigan Stadium Howard King announced different scores from games around the country and the Big Ten on the public address system. The scores of Ohio State or Michigan State would always get a big reaction from the crowd depending on whether they were winning or losing. But one other score always got a huge response, and I always wondered why. The Slippery Rock State Teachers College always got great groans from the Michigan fans if they were behind or a great cheer if they were ahead.

"When I came here, one of the things I was told was that over time this tradition was done some years ago by accident," King confesses. "Apparently somebody handed the announcer this long tickertape, and he just read Slippery Rock and it got this huge crowd reaction. So they started reading it every time.

"When I got here, there was a ticker, so I would get the tape and I would read the score. It always got a crowd reaction. It meant nothing to me, because I was from Wooster, Ohio. I knew about Slippery Rock; it was a great teachers college over in western Pennsylvania, but beyond that it meant nothing to me."

For some reason though, it meant something to the faithful at Michigan Stadium, so King kept reading the Slippery Rock score and getting a great crowd reaction until that fateful day when Michigan changed the method on how they received out-of-town scores.

"When we couldn't get their score every time," King remembers. "I had Art Parker, one of the press box volunteer workers, make a phone call and get their score. That went on for a while until one day when Parker came to me and told me that Slippery Rock didn't want to do it anymore.

"Apparently, they got tired of feeding Michigan the information, because Slippery Rock felt all we did was laugh at them."

That wasn't the case, but that didn't mean Slippery Rock was out of the mix.

"I got to a point where I just didn't do Slippery Rock for a while, but I got bugged about it so much I finally just made up a score. I'd pick out a school and make up a score. I usually had 'em in the second quarter—Slippery Rock 10, Wooster nothing, whatever I could think of," King chuckled. "It was really just to keep the crowd happy. I did that for a while, then I felt it was inappropriate, so I just quit."

Nowadays, the scores are on the big scoreboard, and Slippery Rock doesn't get a mention. It's a shame. Made up or not, it was kind of fun to know how Slippery Rock was doing.

A little gamesmanship

The press box at Michigan Stadium is named after Bob Ufer, and that is very appropriate in my judgment. His years of service in the broadcast booth calling the Michigan games are some of the best years the football program has enjoyed. Part of the reason for that was the unbridled passion and joy with which Ufer spoke about his beloved "Meeechigan Wolverines." Sitting next to Ufer for 31 years in that booth was Jack Lane. Lane was Ufer's stats guy, and he knew how "Ufe" liked to operate when they worked games around the Big Ten.

One time at Memorial Stadium in Minnesota, Ufer and Lane were going through their setup routine in the old wooden press box when the Michigan team came out to run through some drills during what was a normally short Friday workout. The team began to run some plays when Lane noticed coach Bo Schembechler looking up and pointing at the windows of the athletic offices, which were at the end of the field. Ufer and Lane noticed the pressed faces against the glass watching the Wolverines with interest. They turned to see what the Michigan coach would do.

"Bo got the team together," Lane says with a laugh, "and he began sketching out plays in the ground. They were wide-open plays; you know he had guys spread out all over the field. He had three and four wide receivers split out."

As Michigan ran some of these wild plays, Ufer and Lane turn to look at the peeping Toms in the office. There was a flurry of activity.

"They were looking at this and thinking Bo was going to surprise them with this wide-open attack the next day," Lane chuckles. "Of course, it didn't happen."

What happened was Ufer and Lane got a good laugh as they watched the Gopher spies absorb the misinformation.

He wouldn't have it any other way

Every broadcaster has his or her own preferences that make him or her feel comfortable when working a game. In many ways it may be considered superstitious, but as a broadcaster you like to feel just right either at home or on the road to so you can give your best performance. For example, I'll always sit on Frank Beckmann's left when broadcasting Michigan games. He likes it that way, and I like it that way. So wherever we go, I'm always on his left. If I have to crawl over boxes, I am on his left. We've never really spoken about it, that's just the way it is.

Some broadcasters don't like the window of the press box open in the booth if the weather is cold or inclement. Thankfully, Beckmann and I totally agree on this one. The window is always open for the game. Rain, snow, wind, or cold, the window is open. We need to feel the game just like the folks in the stands in order to get the job done. I will tell you that I have worked with some who didn't like it that way, and I have had to broadcast games in a hermetically sealed booth. It was awful. In one instance, I complained enough that we instituted the *pencil rule*. The window would be open wide enough for a No. 2 pencil to slide easily through the opening. It was a minor concession, but enough for me to carry on.

The same proved true for Bob Ufer. "Ufe" loved the windows open, no matter what the weather.

"Bob just could not broadcast a game without the crowd noise," his statistician Jack Lane remembers, "that's why the windows were always open. There were many times when it rained, and the water came in on us, all over the papers and statistics. The ink used to run on the papers, and it was a mess, but Bob wouldn't have it any other way."

This particular preference of Ufer would prove to be very problematic and very expensive for him one year in Iowa. The Wolverines had traveled to Iowa City to take on the Hawkeyes. It had been a couple of years since Michigan had made the trip to Kinnick Stadium and in the interim the University of Iowa had remodeled part of it, including the press box. When Ufer and Lane arrived in the booth the Friday before the game, they found the windows were permanently closed.

"I guess they did it that way because they get a lot of wind and bad weather," Lane explains, "but Bob didn't like it. We expected it to be like it had been before: In the past, we could request from Iowa that they take it out and they would. Bob could then have the open window for the broadcast. Well, this time when we asked the sports information director to get the window removed, he told us they were permanent. They couldn't be taken out. They were locked in place."

This was clearly a problem for Ufer.

"He kept telling us that we had to get rid of the glass," Lane recalls. "He even asked if he could break it!"

Lane told Ufer that breaking the glass wasn't the answer. Lane had another plan; he had previously done business with a company in Cedar Rapids while working his day job. Lane also had gotten their assistant chief engineer a couple of tickets to the Michigan–Iowa game the next day. He told Ufer he'd make a call and see if he couldn't get this situation resolved.

"So, I called this friend of mine at this company," Lane says with a grin, "and they had all sorts of equipment in their shop. Well, I told him about our problem, and he agreed to help us, but he made us promise not to mention his name.

"On Saturday morning, very early, he came down to the stadium and met us. We went up to the press box with a glass-cutter he had brought with him, and we took out all the glass in the booth!"

That solved the problem. Ufer broadcast the game with an open window, and all was well with Michigan football.

But you should also know that he was not about to damage someone's property and just leave town. According to Lane, Ufer was upfront.

"When we left the game, Bob told the Iowa sports information director what we had done," Lane recalls, "and he made sure the guy knew to send him the bill for the window replacement, and Bob paid for the window out of his own pocket."

We knocked them off the air

As the statistics guy for Michigan football broadcasts, Jack Lane has seen a lot. He's seen a swarm of monarch butterflies nearly blot out the sun at Dyche Stadium in Evanston, Illinois, on a Friday afternoon as they migrated to Mexico. Lane swears there were millions of them. He's also seen some of the greatest college football players in history come through the tunnel at Michigan Stadium and seen countless more in stadiums across the country where Michigan traveled. One of the stadiums where Lane has had some of his more memorable moments lies in the Arroyo Seco at the edge of the foothills of the San Gabriel Mountains in Southern California. It's known as the Rose Bowl.

When Lane was working with Bob Ufer, the Rose Bowl facility was just starting to become outdated. The game—"The Granddaddy of Them All"—had become such an event that there wasn't enough room to accommodate all of the media outlets that wanted to cover it. The Rose Bowl had to squeeze broadcast crews and their ever-increasing amounts of equipment into every nook and cranny.

It was this backdrop that Lane and Ufer entered one January as they prepared to broadcast the Rose Bowl back to the Michigan faithful.

"At that time," Lane recalls, "there was only one main press box, and we were put up on the roof of the press box in this wooden booth. They were awful little wooden booths. The only broadcast position in the main press box was the official Rose Bowl broadcast, and the rest of us were put up on the roof.

"One of the things we always had to be aware of was Bob's eyesight. He could not see very well. Around 4:30 p.m. or 5 p.m. at the Rose Bowl, it started to get dark. We knew that with Bob's eyes the way they were, we needed more light in this rickety booth for him to see. So the day before the game, we went out and bought some extension plugs and a lamp with a shield over it that we could hang from the ceiling."

They hung the lamp and got all of the extension cords plugged in despite the lack of outlets in this makeshift booth. The jury-rigged system was tested, and all went well. They were ready for the Rose Bowl.

The next day, all was going very well. The broadcast was flawless, and Ufer was at his bombastic best. All of the makeshift wooden broadcast booths tied together in a row across the roof of the Rose Bowl press box were humming with the voices of announcers sending the game story home—across the country and the globe. As the game continued on into the second half, just as Ufer and Lane had expected, it started to get dark.

No problem, right? The Michigan crew had anticipated the growing darkness.

"In the booth next to us," Lane remembers with a smile, "was the crew from Japan. We could hear them a little during the game through the wall. Well, when it got dark, we threw the switch and our lights worked. Our booth lit up, and Bob could see. But then we heard this commotion next to us. All of a sudden the door to our booth flew open, and a Japanese guy came in screaming at us. We had no idea what he was saying, he was *yelling in Japanese.* We finally figured out that when we plugged in our lights, we had knocked them off the air!

"Bob just kept on talking as the Japanese guy yelled at us. We finally got him quieted down, but Bob never missed a beat. Finally during a timeout we got it figured out, and they got back on the air somehow."

Whatever it took, Ufer was going to get the story back home to Michigan about his beloved Wolverines—even if it took a "power play" over the Japanese, "Ufe" was going to get it done.

No use crying...

S tatistician Jack Lane not only spent 31 years by the side of Bob Ufer, but he continued to be the stat man after Ufer passed away. It was at the Rose Bowl sometime before the first bowl game Frank Beckmann and I ever broadcast that Lane paid the price for his seat between us.

I like to pace and move about when I am a bit nervous before a game, and because this was the first Rose Bowl I had ever broadcast, I was pacing and moving a bit more than normal. Beckmann was busy preparing with his head buried in a press guide, memorizing the last few facts he could squeeze into his memory. The booth at the Rose Bowl was small. We were all kind of stuffed into three chairs that could barely fit across the width of the booth window. Beckmann was thirsty, and he turned and asked me to pass him a soft drink. Because I was standing and pacing, I was more than happy to oblige. I filled a cup to the brim and started to pass it to him. The cup traveled directly over the head of the unaware Jack Lane. Beckmann's hand reached for the cup, but I was not ready for the reach.

The cup fell.

The liquid was expelled in a torrent all over Lane. Both Beckmann and I felt horrible. Lane was soaked. He stayed wet and sticky the entire game.

There were times I think Lane probably deserved hazard pay for occupying the seat between Beckmann and me. But thank the Lord he did, we're both better broadcasters today because of it.

CHAPTER FOUR

Coaches

This isn't BYU

Looking back at 1997, the last time Michigan won the national title, the Wolverines were not rated very highly in the preseason national polls, and the coaching staff had undergone some changes prior to the season.

Although Lloyd Carr was in his third year as head coach, he had elevated two assistants to top jobs on his staff. Jim Herrmann was promoted from linebackers coach to defensive coordinator, and Mike DeBord had been elevated from assistant head coach to offensive coordinator. Charles Woodson won the Heisman Trophy that year, and the team went unbeaten and won the national title, which kind of overshadowed these moves by Coach Carr at the beginning of the season.

Both moves worked out extraordinarily well. Herrmann's defense was aggressive and dominant all year. Michigan's offense, managed by DeBord and led by quarterback Brian Griese, was efficient. It was the offense and DeBord, though, that got the attention of the head coach early in the season.

"That was the first season I called the offense," DeBord remembers, "and it was in our first ballgame. I obviously had a few extra jitters, and I'll never forget I called two passes right in a row, and all of a sudden, right in the middle of a series, I hear from Lloyd, and he says, 'Hey Mike, this is *Michigan,* not BYU!'"

DeBord laughs about the incident now, but a message was sent.

"Right then I knew, the deal was set," DeBord chuckles, "we've got to get back to running the ball."

That wasn't us

Winning a national title, as the Wolverines did in 1997, is a very difficult accomplishment. There are challenges every step along the way. As a matter of fact, Lloyd Carr used the analogy of climbing Mount Everest as the lesson to his team: You must take one step at a time. That season he kept harping at his charges not to look too far ahead, rather, to concentrate on the next step only. The goal each week wasn't the summit; it was only the next game. It was a great motivator for the team, and as it turned out, it worked brilliantly as Michigan went unbeaten.

Coach Carr had gotten the idea for the Mount Everest challenge from a book he had read the previous summer called *Into Thin Air.* It was written by Jon Krakauer, who climbed to the top of Everest and whose party had met with tragedy on their descent. Coach Carr contacted Lou Kasischke, a member of one of the climbing parties on that fateful day. Kasischke, who lives near Ann Arbor, accepted Coach Carr's invitation to speak to the team before the season began about his incredible story. His message was powerful, and it clearly made an impact on the 1997 Wolverines.

During that season, there was one moment when it appeared as though Michigan would stumble, and Everest—or the national title—would be lost. It was in the sixth game against the Iowa Hawkeyes.

Up to that point, the Wolverines' closest game was a seven-point win over Notre Dame. Michigan had been dominant. They had bombed Colorado in the opener 27-3. Baylor then fell 38-3. The Notre Dame win was next and was followed by a 37-0 thrashing of Indiana. Northwestern was next to fall at 23-6. Michigan had risen to fifth in the national polls on October 18 when the 15th-ranked Hawkeyes came to Ann Arbor.

More than 106,000 fans were on hand for the game. Michigan was favored going in, but the first half was a disaster. The Wolverines threw three first-half interceptions. Iowa took advantage, building a lead. Then right before halftime Iowa's Tim Dwight further added to the misery of the gathered Michigan faithful by returning a punt 61 yards for a touchdown. As the Wolverines jogged to the tunnel under the eastern sidelines at Michigan Stadium, they were leaving a mountain behind them. Iowa was confident, they had a 21-7 lead, and they were good. The mountain Michigan had to climb in the second half wasn't Everest, but it was close.

At times like this, a coach has to use his skills as a motivator to keep his team from losing confidence. He must also use his instincts to determine what approach would be best to change the dynamics of the team and the game.

During halftime, Coach Carr picked the perfect approach, although it wasn't what was expected. Mike DeBord was just as frustrated as anyone as he entered the locker room for the halftime break. He was mad because this Michigan team was better than they had played in that first half. DeBord thought Coach Carr was going to be mad, too.

"I thought Lloyd was going to really go after this team," DeBord recalls with a grin. "I really thought he was going to attack the team, the coaches, and everybody else in the room.

"But I'll tell you what. He came into the locker room, and it was probably the best job of a halftime that I've ever seen by a coach. Lloyd came in, and he got the whole team together. He brought all of the coaches together with the team. He was calm, and he said, 'Look, that wasn't us out there in the first half. We're only down by 14 points.' He then paused and looked around at the entire team, and asked, 'Now, is there a man in here who doesn't believe we can come back and win this football game?' Well, you could just feel the energy come out of that. The entire team roared and Lloyd said, 'Okay then, I want everybody to get their poise under control. And let's go back out there and *play by play*, let's get this thing done, one play at a time, let's win it!'"

Michigan did just that. They beat Iowa 28-24 on a late touchdown pass from Brian Griese to Jerame Tuman. The Wolverines marched forward from that game and would not lose the rest of the way. Their season culminated with a 20-14 win over Ohio State. In the Rose Bowl, the Wolverines beat Washington State 21-16 to nail down the national championship. After the Iowa comeback, Michigan beat five ranked teams, three of which were ranked in the top five.

"That halftime of the Iowa game," DeBord concludes, "was just a masterful job of coaching by Lloyd. He did a great job that whole year of keeping the team focused. When the wins started adding up as we got closer and closer to the end, the pressure started mounting. Lloyd took the pressure off of all of the players and coaches by telling everybody to just go out there and have fun."

Just like climbing Mount Everest, Coach Carr made sure he kept everyone's eye on the big prize. And that prize wasn't the summit; it was just the next play.

I was a hurtin' puppy

There are great victories, and then there are great victories. One of the greatest in recent history came against the Minnesota Golden Gophers in 2003.

The 2003 season had been a roller-coaster ride. In game three Michigan bombed Notre Dame 38-0, a win that win catapulted the Wolverines to No. 3 in the polls. In some circles, the win over the Irish put Michigan in the mix for a national title. But the following weeks after a difficult loss at Oregon and a 30-27 loss to Iowa in Iowa City, a team that had been ranked third in the nation, had plummeted to No. 20. And so a disappointed Michigan traveled to Minnesota to take on the unbeaten 17th-ranked Gophers.

Clearly the game with Minnesota was to be a season maker or a season breaker. I was there broadcasting the game with Frank Beckmann for WJR and the Michigan Football Radio Network, and we were caught up in the game as you can imagine. In the early going, Michigan remained in the funk that had traveled with them to Oregon and Iowa. Unbelievably, the Wolverines trailed at halftime 14-0. At the end of three quarters, Minnesota led 28-7. For all intents and purposes, it appeared that it was game, set, and match. You could have called for a fork; Michigan was done.

But in what became the biggest comeback in Michigan history, the Wolverines put on a furious display. It was astonishing! There wasn't a sense of panic, just an incredible sense of urgency that the Wolverines showed on every snap of the ball in the final 15 minutes. They clawed their way back into the game. In the fourth quarter, Michigan scored 31 points. John Navarre hit 15 of 20 passes for 195 yards, *in the quarter!* When Garret Rivas slammed home a 33-yard field goal with 47 seconds left, the Wolverines had taken the lead 38-35. Then to top it off, Markus Curry intercepted the stunned Gophers' last-gasp effort at a Hail Mary pass.

Michigan had won! A season had been saved!

After the game I hurried down to the locker room from the Metrodome press box. I knew it would be a great postgame show. It's one of the real perks of my job that I get to experience the unbridled joy of the team in the locker room after a huge victory. I couldn't wait to get there.

In my mind I was going over what questions I could ask coach Lloyd Carr to bring out the emotions I knew he and the team had to be feeling.

As I arrived, I was struck by the noise. Nobody was talking in a normal tone of voice. Everyone was yelling. Players were pounding each other on the back, screaming with glee, and then hugging. Coaches were picking their way between the discarded shoulder pads, pieces of adhesive tape, and shoes on the floor to hug players and each other. It was a beautiful sight, and I stood there inside the locker room doors, about 10 feet from the tunnel corridor.

Directly across from me was the open entryway to the bathrooms. As the bedlam started to subside in the locker room, I could hear someone in the bathroom getting violently ill. I mean we are talking the dry heaves!

As Coach Carr stood on a chair to address the team, everyone quieted down, except in the bathroom, where the retching continued. Navarre and Carl Diggs, the two captains got up on chairs and addressed the team. There was cheering and even louder yelling as the celebration continued. But the retching also continued. The team then stood as one, and throwing their fists into the air for emphasis, they sang a hearty, emotional rendition of "The Victors." As they finished the song, I noticed the retching had stopped.

As I waited by my live radio hookup to interview Coach Carr on the postgame show, I caught the eye of trainer Paul Schmidt.

"Someone in there is very sick," I told him, pointing to the bathroom.

In the excitement of the win, I think I was the only one who had noticed the problem.

Schmidt checked, and moments later he emerged from the bathroom with a hand under the elbow of Michigan quarterbacks coach Scott Loeffler. Schmidt seemed to be steadying Coach Loeffler. Coach Loeffler's face was kind of a mix between beet red with a tinge of green. He did not look good. Schmidt nodded at me as the two walked by, indicating that he had the situation in hand. At the time, I guessed that the comeback victory had been so stressful for Coach Loeffler while coaching from the press box that his stomach acid had overcooked and caused his problems. I was glad he was in the trainer's hands.

It was only later that I found the true source of his ailment, and it wasn't exactly as I had pictured it.

"Unfortunately, I had a terrible habit of chewing tobacco at that time," Coach Loeffler confesses. "And in between every single call in that game, I think I must have stuffed another half a tin in my mouth. I think I went through three tins of Copenhagen.

"I'll bet I swallowed at least a can and a half of the stuff. After the game, I was emotionally drained. The players were just great leading us back to victory. [Offensive coordinator Terry] Malone did a great job putting us in position to give our players the chance to win. The defense made a great interception for a score. And all I remember was walking across the field thinking what a tremendous win. I was part of the greatest comeback in Michigan history, and then I proceeded to throw up all the way up the tunnel to the locker room."

"[But] I think I might have gotten sick regardless of the Copenhagen. I get emotionally attached to those games. I think a lot of people who were fans may have gotten sick over that one. If you watched that game, it was up, down, a roller-coaster ride."

And by the way, the story also has a silver lining.

"When I got to the locker room, I kept throwing up during Lloyd's and the players' speeches," Coach Loeffler says. "I was a hurtin' puppy. I can tell you this, though, *I will never forget that day!* It was the day of Michigan's greatest comeback victory, and it was the day I quit chewing tobacco."

(Author's note: Scott Loeffler is a wonderful young coach. He is a gifted and tireless worker and can flat-out coach quarterbacks. He is a huge asset to the Michigan staff, with or without tobacco chewing.)

It was supposed to be off-tackle

Like the Minnesota comeback win, if you are a Wolverine fan, you know where you were that day in 1991 when Michigan beat the Irish 24-14 in Ann Arbor. It was the game that Desmond Howard made one of the greatest catches in Michigan history. Diving into the end zone—parallel to the ground—on a pass that he had no chance to catch, somehow Howard pulled it in. It was a stunning play. It was the key to the Wolverine win. It also was instrumental in launching Howard's Heisman Trophy run. It was a magical moment for Michigan fans everywhere. If you were in the Stadium, it was even better.

If you were on the sidelines watching this play unfold as coach Gary Moeller was, the play was much different. For Moeller, it was his second year as head coach. He had lost to Notre Dame in his first year at South Bend by four points. It was a game Michigan should have won, but inside the last two minutes, Notre Dame, as they so often do at home, found a way to snatch a victory away.

So for Coach Moeller and his Wolverines, this was a huge game, and this play call was even bigger. It was a fourth-and-one situation. It was like going all in at a high-stakes poker game.

"[Quarterback] Elvis [Grbac] was going to run off-tackle or throw a hitch pass to Desmond," Moeller remembers with clarity. "Desmond was going to run down the field five yards and turn around, because they've got off coverage on him. If he's in single coverage and he's out there by himself, Elvis can look and see the defensive back playing off and he can hit Desmond on this five-yard hitch, and we've got the first down."

The problem with the plan was that Notre Dame didn't cooperate.

"As Elvis is into the snap count," Coach Moeller recalls with a smile, "the next thing you know, Notre Dame isn't in the coverage we thought they'd be in. They camouflaged it just enough, and Elvis checks to the pass! The cornerback then rolled up on Desmond. When he rolls up late like that, you can't throw the hitch, and Desmond is taught to run the fade. So when Elvis fades back to throw, he was expecting to throw the hitch, and he sees Desmond take off!"

Imagine all of this is happening in an instant. Coach Moeller can only watch. It is out of his hands, but when he saw the Notre Dame cornerback roll up on Howard, he thought it was over.

"I was thinking to myself, 'Oh crap!'" he recalls. "But those kids had worked on that pass a lot. They could pull it off. It was a beautiful throw, and what a wonderful catch by Desmond. That was a *great* play in a *great* game against a *great* team."

I won't argue with you on that one, and I doubt anyone else will, either.

Blue was for sky, it meant pass

One of the most innovative coaches I've ever met is Gary Moeller. He loves spending time in the staff meeting room, designing plays. Whether it was on offense or defense, Mo would tinker with something until he got it just right. As an assistant at Michigan under Bo Schembechler or as the head coach when he replaced Schembechler, Coach Moeller was always thinking, plotting, and planning a better mousetrap as it related to his football team.

As these plans came rolling out of Coach Moeller's imagination, there had to be a way to take them to the field and incorporate them in the game. These plans were a bit complicated at times and required some cryptic spoken signals by the quarterback or a linebacker as the team was at the line of scrimmage before the snap of the ball. Over the years as the game progressed and got more complicated, the code words got more and more odd.

For example, I will go back to my playing days at Michigan Stadium from 1969 to 1971. Back in those days, we didn't have a lot of checks, or audibles, called at the line of scrimmage. In most instances, the play we called in the huddle was the play we ran at the line of scrimmage. Now as a lineman, we had different ways to block the same play depending on what defense the opponent showed us. As a strong tackle, I would yell out a number—the signal—when I recognized the defensive front. Either two, four, six, or eight was used to alert the guard and end on my side of the ball how we would attack the defense based on their alignment. When the ball was going away from our side, I would still yell out a number, which was a *dummy call,* so the defensive player across from me wouldn't get too wise and think that every time I yelled, "Six!" he was going to get double-teamed. Anyway, it was a pretty simple system.

As the game changed, even from year to year, Schembechler and his staff had to evolve to give us the best opportunity to succeed. After a while opposing coaches used to overload their defense based on our position on the field (left hash or right hash) or the formation our offense showed them. It got to the point that running a play into the strength of the defense was not very efficient if the other coach anticipated correctly what we were planning to run. So we came up with a system of checks at the line of scrimmage that was very simple. It revolved around our snap count. At that time the standard snap count had the quarterback set up under center and yell, "Hit!" When the play was called in the huddle and the quarterback said the snap count was first sound, we took off on "Hit!" If the play wasn't on the first sound, the next word in the snap count sequence was a color, then a number, and then the word, "Go!" If the snap count was on one, we would take off on the first "Go!" If the snap count was on two, we would take off on the second "Go!" and so on.

The automatics came in during the color and number phase of the snap count. Most of our checks at the line of scrimmage were right or left checks. We rarely ran a run or pass audible. When we did go to an automatic at the line, the quarterback's call in the huddle would consist of the formation set up, the play number, and the snap count. Then we'd break the huddle and get to the line of scrimmage. When we broke, we knew that we were running a sweep or off-tackle play, but if during the snap count he yelled the active color, which was decided before the game, it signaled a change in play, and the next thing he yelled was the new call. For example, if a left sweep was called in the huddle toward the wide side of the field, and the quarterback saw the defense shifted that way, his snap count sequence would be "Hit, (pause) Blue, 28, Go, Go!" That told us the play had changed from a left sweep, to a right sweep.

It was relatively simple but effective for the time. As the game has progressed, defenses and offenses have become more sophisticated, requiring more complicated systems. In today's modern-day game, if you don't have the ability to change on the fly, you are in a world of hurt. Well, Coach Moeller was one of the most inventive and yet understandable coaches at creating the change on the fly. I can't tell you how many practices I watched when he was the defensive coordinator, and I would hear a linebacker yell something like, "Omaha!" or "Husker!" and immediately five or six guys would shift their positions, putting them in a better spot to make a play.

On offense it was the same story, and Coach Moeller's methods for coming up with these codes were ingenious.

"We ran a lot of run/pass checks," he confides. "We used the words 'Bo' or 'Wolverine' for our checks. When we said, 'Bo!' for a check at the line of scrimmage, it meant we were going to run an off-tackle play, because Bo [Schembechler] loved to run the ball. 'Wolverine' meant we were checking to a pass."

It was enough of a mystery for the opponent to have trouble figuring it out, yet easy enough for the Michigan kids to immediately know what was coming and change their assignments before the snap.

Coach Moeller was a master at the process, and it didn't stop with "Bo" and "Wolverine."

"Sometimes we used 'Blue' and 'Maize,' too," he chuckles. "If the quarterback came to the line and gave the live color, the guys knew a check was coming. If he said 'Blue' or 'Maize,' it meant a pass. 'Blue' and 'Maize' go together, and blue is the color of the sky, so that was our code for 'pass.' Anytime we used 'Blue' or 'Maize,' we threw the ball. We wanted to make the check at the line, so we could go and attack the weak spot of the defense."

Coach Gary Moeller is an innovative and a brilliant coach.

All football teams do this to get an edge on their opponent, and it's even more intense in today's game. Moeller did it as well as any coach. In his five years as the head coach at Michigan, Moeller won three Big Ten titles. He was 4-1 in bowl appearances, and his teams averaged more than 31 points per game during his tenure as head coach.

I would venture to say Coach Moeller checked into the right stuff more often than not.

The return game helped him

In the history of Michigan football, only three men have ever won the Heisman Trophy. If you are a Michigan fan, I am sure you know the three Michigan players who have captured the top honor in college football. It should also be noted that only three coaches in Wolverine football history have coached Heisman winners, and they are Fritz Crisler, Gary Moeller, and Lloyd Carr. For Moeller and Carr, their Heisman players were not the odds-on favorites to win the trophy when their magical years began. Yet both coaches put these talented players in the best positions to excel, and that helped them reach the pinnacle.

Howard had an incredible season in 1991. I was in my 12th year of hosting *Michigan Replay,* the coach's television show, and Coach Moeller was in his second year as head coach. One Saturday night, later in the season, after taping the show, Coach Moeller and I were privately talking about the afternoon's game, and I mentioned that I thought Howard was making a great run at the Heisman.

"Do you really think so?" he asked.

He seemed a bit surprised.

"Who else is out there that is having the kind of year that Desmond is?" I responded with astonishment.

Even 13 years later he remembers the conversation.

"Well, I was a little surprised, because that thing [the Heisman Trophy] is so hard to win," he explains. "The thing that really helped Desmond that year was the return game. And he didn't hurt his chances when he promoted himself against Ohio State."

(Moeller was referring to the Ohio State game of 1991 when Howard struck a Heisman Trophy-like pose in the end zone after he returned a Buckeye punt for a touchdown.)

So many factors are involved in a player's march toward an award like the Heisman, and many of those factors can only be considered fate. In Howard's Heisman year, it should be remembered that in the opening game of the season, his bookend wide receiver teammate, Derrick Alexander, injured his knee and was lost for the season. That was a big factor in Howard getting more opportunities to shine.

"Think about it," Coach Moeller recalls. "When Alexander got hurt against Boston College, our other wide receiver was Yale Van Dyne."

Although Van Dyne was a fine receiver, he was not a guy who struck fear in the hearts of too many Big Ten defensive coordinators. He certainly didn't present the threat that either Alexander or Howard did. Van Dyne played very well that year and made some big plays, but it was clear that Howard had become the go-to big-play guy, and Coach Moeller had to scheme Howard into a position to make more plays than they had originally planned because of the injury to Alexander.

"We did the same thing with Desmond that we did with Anthony [Carter] years before," Moeller says matter-of-factly. "We put the formation into the boundary and then lined up our best wideout, all the way wide, out there by himself. If the defense doesn't double-cover him out there, that wide receiver has all kinds of room. Desmond, Anthony, Mercury Hayes, Amani Toomer, they all were able to run that corner route against single coverage. And then," Mo grins while thinking about the strategy, "if the defense put two people out there to cover the wide guy, they couldn't cover the off-tackle run to the weak side. We ran that play and blew it up in that big area where our back had two-thirds of the field to run in!"

All of this happened because of events that occurred outside the influence of Desmond Howard. He certainly benefited greatly because of these events, but winning the Heisman, like Coach Moeller says, is a hard thing to do. Injuries and fate aside, the player who wins it has got to have the talent to get it done, too.

"I'll tell you one thing for sure," Coach Moeller remembers, "Desmond really played hard that year."

Howard's Heisman was the second in Wolverine history. Not since Tom Harmon won the trophy in 1940 had a Wolverine received the honor. A span of 51 years had passed between the first two winners who wore Maize and Blue. Seven years later, Michigan would get its third Heisman when Charles Woodson was named the winner after the 1997 season.

I saw it on TV again last night

If there is one game in the coaching career of Gary Moeller that he wishes would just be erased from history, it is the 1994 Michigan versus Colorado game. It was a game that Michigan should have won. In my mind it was a game that Michigan would have won except for the last play. That last play. To add a twist to a historical phrase from Franklin Delano Roosevelt, it was a play that will live in infamy.

Michigan entered the game as the fourth-ranked team in the country; Colorado came to the game as the seventh-ranked team in the country. For 59 minutes and 55 seconds these two titans played a great football game. But in the last five seconds this game turned into a nightmare for Michigan, their fans, and Coach Moeller.

The Wolverines scored 17 third-quarter points to take a commanding 26-14 lead. The last touchdown had come on a 65-yard bomb from Todd Collins to Amani Toomer. That lead stood up until Colorado's Rashan Salaam scored with just 2:16 left in the game. When Michigan got the ball back on the ensuing kickoff, the game appeared to be over. But the Wolverines could only kill two minutes of the clock. Colorado got the ball back on their 15-yard line with 15 seconds left. No chance, right? *Wrong!*

After a completion out to the 36-yard line, Colorado had time for only one more play, but they were 64 yards away from the end zone. They would try the Hail Mary pass, but this play would have to be more than just one prayer, it would have to be a whole rosary to rescue the game for the Buffalos. Incredibly, the rosary was answered. Kordell Stewart somehow launched a pass that had to carry 70 yards in the air, and even though Michigan cornerback Ty Law tipped the ball, as it fell toward the ground Colorado's Michael Westbrook was in the right spot at the right time and made the catch. Colorado won the game 27-26. It was stunning.

I can never remember Michigan Stadium being that quiet. Everyone was in shock.

On the Michigan bench, no one was more shocked than Coach Moeller. To this very day, you can hear the disappointment and hurt in his voice as he tries to discuss that last play.

"I don't know what happened," Coach Moeller says with disgust. "To this very day, I'm not sure what happened. I think a couple of our guys didn't go as hard as they should have. Their guy, Westbrook, was lazy and got down the field late, and we didn't get any pressure...."

Moeller's voice trails off. It was as if he was still looking for an answer, almost as if he were replaying everyone's position on the field and remembering in slow motion how the play unfolded.

He didn't deserve this kind of loss, and neither did his team.

Whatever happened, it was a classical comedy of errors and luck as far as Coach Moeller is concerned that resulted in the Colorado miracle.

"We may have missed the jam on some of the receivers," Moeller grudgingly remembers, "but we got the jam on the guy who caught the ball. I mean Westbrook was the *last* guy down the gol-dang field! To figure out one of those plays is so hard. I mean, you can name a number of things that caused it, like, not enough pressure, or the defender didn't go up to bat the ball down like he should have.

"You know, it's not luck, but it *is* luck, to a certain extent. I mean those plays don't happen too often. That day, it happened to us. It was just a sick, sick day."

After all these years, he is still looking for some kind of answer why this happened to his team. However, his most vivid memory about the incredible moment isn't about what it did to him; it's about how it affected his team.

"Our kids were waiting to celebrate," Coach Moeller says with disappointment. "That's the hardest part about that game and that play. It really taught us about the mindset that you have to have in football. You have to play every play to the end. Every play at every moment in the game is important.

"I mean even before that play ever happened, we had the ball, and we got a damn penalty. Any way we can get three or four seconds more off that clock, we win!"

The finish to Kordell Stewart's Hail Mary was so big that it has followed Coach Moeller around, much to his dismay. After leaving Michigan, he moved on to a very distinguished career in the National Football League as the head coach of the Detroit Lions and as an assistant coach for the Chicago Bears. Well, during his time as an assistant in Chicago, the Bears just happened to sign Stewart—the man whose arm threw the bullet that killed Michigan hopes that day—as their starting quarterback. Coach Moeller, who is known for his likeability, and Stewart hit it off despite Stewart's good-natured ribbing about that infamous play.

"You know, the last couple of years I was with the Bears," Coach Moeller laughs, "Kordell would come into the office about every other day and find me and say, 'Hey Mo, I saw it on TV again last night.' He's a good kid."

The old adage is: Time heals all wounds. For Gary Moeller and the rest of us, I hope time starts hurrying up.

Erroneously reported

Since 1982, there have been a lot of Anthony Carter stories that have floated around Ann Arbor and the Michigan football program. What you may *not* have heard about Carter was the time he left school, and there was a concern he wasn't coming back!

The most commonly reported version of this event indicates that early in fall practice of Carter's freshman year, he was missing from practice, and head coach Bo Schembechler sent assistant coach Bob Thornbladh, who was the receivers coach at the time, out to look for him.

"That is an erroneous report," Coach Thornbladh chuckled. "Let me go back and tell you the whole story."

The whole story starts at the very beginning of Carter's Michigan career. Coach Thornbladh recalls what an impression Carter made the first practice where he caught every overthrown ball. The coaches were blown away by his ability to accelerate and his amazing game speed. In the coaches' locker room after that practice, there was a buzz of excitement about Carter and what it might mean for the team. When Coach Schembechler entered, he turned to the gathered coaching staff.

"Men, we've got something special," he said prophetically. "We've got a player like we've never had. We may not know how to pass, and we may not know what we're doing, but I'm telling you, this kid is special."

Carter was put on the fast track, and Coach Thornbladh and quarterbacks coach Don Nehlen began grilling him on Xs and Os during the morning practice of two-a-days to speed up the learning process and get him ready to play for the season. In response to every question, Carter mumbled an answer, but the coaches didn't think anything of it because Carter was very shy.

After a break, Coach Thornbladh and the rest of the staff were getting ready to start the afternoon practice when they looked out at all of the players stretching and noticed that Carter was missing.

"Where the hell is Carter?" Coach Schembechler barked.

"He's not here," Coach Thornbladh replied.

The silence was deafening as the head coach stared out at the field.

"Bo didn't say a word to me," Coach Thornbladh recalls years later. "He would never excuse a coach from practice to go chase a player. Bo's attitude was if a player didn't want to come to practice and play at Michigan, that's fine. Playing at Michigan is a privilege, and if you don't come to practice, you will no longer be afforded that privilege, so you're gone!"

Coach Thornbladh decided it was up to him.

"Coach, I'm going to go find him," he said.

Coach Thornbladh grabbed strength coach Mike Gittleson and left the practice facility to check out the dorms. They figured Carter might have overslept. They checked his room and scoured the halls—but he wasn't there. Then they checked the

Anthony Carter got away from a lot of people—including coach Bob Thornbladh.

basketball courts—not there either. They searched all over campus—nothing.

They returned to the field and with practice now over, Coach Schembechler told them to keep looking.

Coach Thornbladh and Coach Gittleson then tried the airport because there was a night flight to Fort Lauderdale, Carter's hometown. The two coaches hightailed it to the gate—still no Carter. They decided to check out the video arcade—and there they found their lost wide receiver.

(Coach Thornbladh usually jokes that Coach Schembechler had told him to tackle Carter when the recievers coach located the missing player and that he tried to but missed 10 times.)

The men pulled him aside to talk.

"Before you leave, Bo wants to talk to you," Coach Thornbladh told him.

They found a pay phone and dialed Coach Schembechler's number. They put the freshman on the phone.

There was a pause as Carter listened to the coach.

"Uh huh," he muttered. "Uh huh. Uh huh. Okay."

He hung up the receiver and turned to the two older men.

"What did Bo say, Anthony?" Coach Thornbladh asked.

"Bo said I could go home."

So the two coaches left him at the airport, and the wide receiver got on a plane to Florida.

When Coach Thornbladh got home, he called Coach Schembechler.

"Why did you tell Anthony to leave?" he asked.

"I didn't tell him he could leave!" the head coach screamed at his assistant.

They wasted no time in contacting their recruiters in Florida who found Carter at home and talked him into calling the coaching staff. Eventually they convinced him to come back.

"He told us he was just a little homesick and that he was going to come back," Coach Thornbladh remembers with a laugh. "Then he asked us when picture day was so he could be back for that."

The rest, as they say, is history. Maybe we all owe Coach Thornbladh, or "Blade" as he is more widely known, a high-five for leaving practice and tracking Carter down. Those years between 1979 and 1982 wouldn't have been nearly as much fun without No. 1 out there making his magic happen at Michigan Stadium.

The myth of national championships

I n my humble opinion, Bo Schembechler is one of the great coaches in Michigan football history. I may be considered biased by some because I happened to have played for him, but that shouldn't discount my opinion—it should enhance it.

There are critics out there, though, who on occasion criticize Coach Schembechler for certain anomalies in his coaching record. They point to his record in bowl games and the fact that he never won a national title while at Michigan as some kind of criteria that allow them to suggest he was something other than great. I have long battled these critics and will continue to do so as long as I am able. There are countless factors that determine whether one is fortunate enough to be considered great. In the football arena, Coach Schembechler has met the criteria and surpassed them. His former players' and coaches' lives have all been positively affected thanks to their relationship with him. His success goes far beyond the winning and the losing. Sadly, critics can't see beyond the records, and Coach Schembechler gets a bum rap because of a bowl record or a trumped-up quasi-national championship.

There are others who feel the same way. Some of these supporters know far more football than I do and have spent a great deal of their lives in the business of football. One of these people is Bob Thornbladh. He played for Coach Schembechler in the early 1970s. As a matter of fact, he and I were teammates on the 1971 Wolverine squad. He went on to become an assistant at Michigan with Coach Schembechler for six years. Coach Thornbladh was with Coach Schembechler for some of the so-called bowl failures and national championship misses, and he has very strong opinions about those who doubt the greatness of the man we know as "Bo."

"I get mad about it when critics point out that Bo never won a national championship," he says with conviction. "The fact of the matter is *no one* has won a national championship. Even recently, with the BCS, you can argue that a true national champion has never been decided because we don't have a play-off system. They may play a game called the national title game, but it really isn't!

"Back when Bo coached, there were no playoff systems either. National championships were not won on the field. National championships were *awarded*.

"The team we had in 1980," "Blade" adds with more gusto, "with John Wangler, Mel Owens, Ed Muransky, Bubba Paris, Anthony Carter, and Butch Woolfolk, and guys like that.... We would have beaten anybody. We did go out and beat Washington in the Rose Bowl. No one would have beaten us."

That team was considered one of Coach Schembechler's best. They finished the year with a 10-2 record. Early losses to Notre Dame and South Carolina in weeks two and three of the season cost Michigan in the polls, but they won their last nine games in a row and finished the year ranked fifth in the country. I've heard others, including Coach Schembechler, say by the end of that season, that team was as good as any in the nation.

I will add to Coach Thornbladh's argument by pointing out the 1985 Michigan team. They finished the season with a 10-1-1 record. The loss was to Iowa in Iowa City 12-10, and the tie was with Illinois in Champaign. Michigan closed the year with wins over 12th-ranked Ohio State and eighth-ranked Nebraska in the Fiesta Bowl. At the end of that season, I would have put that Michigan squad out there against any other team and taken my chances. They were as good as anybody else in the country, but that's not how national title politics work.

Coach Thornbladh points out that Coach Schembechler's integrity and interest in the students who played the game have also worked against him.

"Bo, of course, is adamantly opposed to a national playoff," he adds, "because he thinks it would hurt the kids academically. And he doesn't want to add too much pressure on them. But I'll tell you this, when they argue about who won the national championship, it's a moot point, because no one has won it on the field. It is *awarded,* not won! In my opinion, Bo had several teams that would have competed very favorably in any national playoff, and he'd probably have two or three titles in his pocket. As it is, he just goes down as the greatest guy and greatest coach who ever lived anyway!"

Well said, "Blade," well said.

CHAPTER FIVE

The Kicking Game

That's my legacy

There is probably no bigger rivalry in college football than Michigan versus Ohio State. Because of the rivalry, events and plays that occur during these games take on even more significance. The stakes are so high and the interest so intense, that a big play or a big mistake can make or break a player's legacy.

For example, Mike Lantry was an excellent placekicker for the Wolverines in the early 1970s. It was his misfortune to be the pivotal player in the outcome of a pair of Michigan–Ohio State games, and neither went Michigan's way.

In 1973 the Wolverines and Buckeyes had battled nearly 60 minutes at Michigan Stadium and nothing had been decided. The score was knotted at 10-10. In the closing seconds, Lantry trotted onto the field to win it for Michigan. He would be attempting a 58-yard field goal. The kick was majestic, high, and long, but at the last moment it moved ever so slightly left of the left upright. No good. Game over. The infamous 10-10 tie.

The next day the Big Ten athletic directors voted to send Ohio State to the Rose Bowl despite both teams having identical records and the Buckeyes having gone to Pasadena the year before. It was a vote that Bo Schembechler is bitter about to this day. And it was a kick that Lantry has had to live with for the rest of his life.

The next year fate came back and sat on the shoulders of Lantry again. It was in the season finale versus Ohio State again. The Wolverines were undefeated; Ohio State had lost just once. The Rose Bowl and the Big Ten title were on the line.

The situation at the close of that game is indelibly etched into Lantry's memory.

"Ohio State couldn't get past our 25-yard line," Lantry remembers, "but their kicker had kicked four field goals to give them a 12-10 lead. There were about 16 seconds remaining, and I came out for a 37-yard attempt."

The kick, if good, would have won the game. If you were watching on TV or at the Horseshoe in Columbus, you probably felt the same way Lantry felt as the ball soared through the Ohio sky.

"To this day, I think it was good," Lantry says flatly. "You can go ask Bo [Schembechler] and he'll say the same thing. Unfortunately, that's not what the ref saw."

What the referee saw was a high kick above the upright. It was a judgment call, and based on the delay, he may not have been absolutely sure himself.

"To be honest with you, I've never seen the replay and don't really care to," Lantry explains. "But from my memory, and that of my holder Tom Drake, we all saw it the same way. It was good!"

It was at that point that Lantry realized there was a problem.

"It was kind of a delayed call, because the referees came running out from under the goalpost, and it seemed like an eterni-

Mike Lantry was a superb kicker although he is unfairly remembered for his misses and not his makes.

ty of a delay, and then they waved it off at the last second," he remembers.

"I've never been bitter about the decision. Don't get me wrong, it was heartbreaking for me, and for my teammates, because we were 10-1 and ranked No. 5 in the nation in the final polls, and we were just sitting home watching Ohio State go to the Rose Bowl."

Two Ohio State games, two missed game-winning kicks. Lantry has admitted it was devastating to him, but as he moved forward in his life, he has not let the two missed kicks define him or his career at Michigan.

"I was a few years older when I was in school," Lantry says. "I had served in Vietnam. For whatever reasons, I just moved on from those misses.

"I remember the athletic department getting a little irritated at me. I was getting tons of mail from people who wanted to tell me how sorrowful they were for me. They just had to reach out and tell me how badly they felt for me."

Although those letters gave Lantry a lift, there was something in his character and what Michigan football had taught him that wouldn't allow his misfortune to stay with him.

"Certainly, I was extremely disappointed. It hurt for a while," he admits, "but I guess it's just not in my nature to hang on to it. I got on with my life and tried to draw some strength from it.

"When I left after the 1974 season, I was third in all-time scoring. I held virtually every field goal record that they had. I am still in the record books as the first Michigan kicker to ever kick a 50-yard field goal. But the truth is, to just be a part of Michigan and a part of some of the great teams that I played on makes me feel very grateful."

(Also remember back in 1972 against the Purdue Boilermakers when Lantry walked into the game with a minute left and drilled a 30-yard field goal to give Michigan a 9-6 win. At the time, the Wolverines were 9-0 and heading into a showdown with Ohio State. Without Lantry, that 1972 matchup with the Buckeyes would have lost some of its luster had Michigan gone into the game with a tie the week before.)

"I am very proud of what I accomplished here, but unfortunately I'll always be remembered for those two kicks that I missed," Lantry laments. "That's my legacy."

I didn't think I'd get a shot

The kicking game can bring disappointment, and it can also bring great joy. While Mike Lantry suffered through two missed kicks in some very high-profile games, a youngster named J.D. Carlson had a much different fate in 1989 in the Rose Bowl against the Bruins of UCLA.

Carlson was very young, and it was his first year as the Wolverine kicker, having won the job in early fall camp. He was taking over for Mike Gillette, who had distinguished himself in previous years but had graduated. Carlson wasn't exactly at his most confident as he entered the UCLA game, and the reason was the previous week's game against Notre Dame.

"Remember," Carlson explains, "that Notre Dame game was the game Rocket Ismail returned two kickoffs for touchdowns. I also missed an extra point in that game and tried an onside kick that was pretty much the worst ever in the history of football."

So it was a less than confident Carlson entering only his second career game as Michigan's starting kicker at the Rose Bowl in Pasadena, California. Surprisingly, it was UCLA who helped Carlson gain his confidence back during the contest.

"I did get a chance to kick a couple field goals in the first half," Carlson says, "and UCLA called two timeouts at the end of the first half to try and ice me on my second field goal. They knew I was inexperienced and playing in only my second game, but I made them both. I made another one in the third quarter, so I was feeling pretty good about myself heading into the end of the game, but I really didn't think I was going to have a shot. We were down by eight with maybe five or six minutes left."

UCLA had pretty much controlled the game. But as fate would have it, a late turnover by UCLA turned momentum around in Michigan's favor.

Carlson now was going to get his shot.

"When Elvis [Grbac] drove us down and got a touchdown to Derrick Walker, we were back in it," Carlson continues with a chuckle. "When the two-point conversion failed, I knew I was going to have to go out there and kick an onside kick.

"Onside kicks are just one of those things. You can practice them, but it doesn't really mean that much. I just put it up there as best I could, and Vada [Murray] pulled it down. You can't plan something like that; it just worked out that way. I couldn't have asked for it to be any better."

In reality, it was a perfect onside kick. Murray caught it on a dead sprint, chest high right on the sideline in front of the UCLA bench.

"J.D. had the hard part," Murray says. "He had to make sure that ball popped up in the air. I had the easy part. All I had to do was catch it and not drop it. It was probably one of the best onside kicks I've ever seen."

The impact of that recovered onside kick might have been a season-saver.

"I think it was the turning point in the game. We should have lost that game," Murray explains. "But it just proves the point that you play until the clock says zero. You can never give up in football or in any other sport. One turnover can make a difference."

The UCLA turnover sure made a difference in this game, but it wasn't in the Michigan win column yet. Carlson remembers that he was brought back to reality moments after the euphoria of Murray's recovery of the onside kick had worn off.

"Before I even made it back to the sideline, I was realizing I needed to keep warm and get ready for a game-winning kick.

"Thankfully," Carlson sighed, "Elvis drove us down in close. It was just a 25-yard field goal. So, it was pretty much a chip shot for me."

Still, for a game winner, 25 yards can be a long way. Veterans have missed them before, but Carlson says he had experience around him that made the difference.

"I had Ken Sollum as my holder," Carlson relates. "He'd been the holder for Mike Gillette the year before. Steve Everritt was the snapper, and he was pretty much one of the best snappers who has ever played. So it was really easy for me to go in there, go numb, and just let the mechanics flow."

The mechanics flowed into a perfect field goal and an improbable come-from-behind 24-23 Wolverine victory. The celebration was immediate and intense. Carlson, who was not a large young man, found himself in the middle of it. His escape from injury in the joyous pile of teammates may have been as remarkable as his game-winning kick.

"I showed the tape of that to my wife years later," Carlson laughs, "and she said, 'Oh my God, are you at the bottom of that pile?' Actually, I had kind of snuck out to the side, so I didn't get piled on. But believe me, it felt great, especially since I had not held up my end of the bargain in the first game for the team. So to come through for all these guys who had worked so hard was great."

I wanted to make a play

One of the greatest kickers in Wolverine history was Monte Robbins. He didn't have any dramatic kicks that won games in the final seconds because he was a punter. But don't discount him as a real force for the Wolverines in the mid-1980s.

To this very day, Robbins is ranked first, second, and third in the Michigan record books in single-season punting average. He averaged more than 43 yards a punt in those years. Only one other punter in Michigan history has averaged better than 43 yards over the course of the season, and Robbins did it three times! He was the defense's best friend in those years.

But one time Robbins decided to not put his best foot forward and took things into his own hands. Michigan was facing Illinois two weeks after a disappointing last-second 12-10 loss to Iowa, which had broken a five-game winning streak that had Michigan ranked No. 2 in the nation.

"Yeah, it was Illinois," Robbins recalls, "the game ended in a 3-3 tie. I was in there to punt on a fourth-and-22 at one point in the game, and there was an Illinois guy who kept coming in at me hard from the left side when I had punted the three or four times before. I knew I could beat him. The one thing I failed to do was look at the scoreboard and see what yard line we were on, and the down and distance. Just a little minor mistake.

"I really wanted to make a play, and besides, the wind was blowing right in my face!" Robbins chuckles. "I thought at the risk of not making a first down, I'll probably hit a lousy punt anyway, so I was going to run it."

From inside his 25-yard line, Robbins took off and ran the ball. Imagine the shock head coach Bo Schembechler felt on the sideline. He had *not* called for a fake punt. It was all Robbins. Luckily, he made the first down, not by much, but he did make it.

When Robbins returned to the bench, there was obvious euphoria. The team was really fired up. It got the Wolverines out of trouble and gave the offense an opportunity to turn field position around against the Illlini. But Robbins knew it wasn't over until he spoke with Coach Schembechler. Working his way through the team as they patted him on the back and hugged him, he made his way to the head coach. Upon arriving at his side, Robbins remembers he got a typical Schembechler response.

"Bo said," Robbins recalls with a laugh, "'If you didn't make that first down, I hope you would have known well enough to keep on running!'"

It was at sea level

Punter Monte Robbins is also in the record books for individual record-breaking punts. He holds the record for the longest punt in Michigan history, an 82-yarder against Hawaii, and he is third on the same list with a 78-yard bomb against Michigan State.

It is the record 82-yarder that is unique for a couple of reasons. First, Robbins says he was struggling the night he set the record, and secondly, the Hawaii return man helped him out.

"I had been kicking them relatively short that day," Robbins says with a grin, "and I think the return guy moved up on me a little bit. I just happened to catch that one just right. Well, it went way over the guy's head, and on the artificial surface it kept bouncing. Yeah, I did get some roll out of it. I have to admit that, but I did hit it pretty well.

"Remember, it was in Hawaii, so I kicked it at sea level. I didn't have the elevation thing going for me."

That's true, but it still was one heck of a kick. It was 1982 when he hammered that record-breaking kick, and no one has come close since.

CHAPTER SIX

Offensive Line

It was dead freaking quiet!

M ichigan Stadium clearly has an emotional impact on almost all of the people who have played there. But sometimes a road win away from Michigan Stadium is a special moment, and that is the case with one of Michigan's best offensive linemen ever, Mike Kenn.

It was 1976, Michigan had been ranked No. 1 in the country for most of the year until an upset loss to Purdue 16-14 in their ninth game of the year. As Kenn and Michigan entered the season finale against Ohio State, they had climbed back up to the No. 2 spot in the national polls. The Buckeyes were ranked No. 8. It was a typical showdown game between the two best teams in the Big Ten.

The two teams raged at each other for the first 30 minutes, and neither gained any ground. It was scoreless at halftime in a sold-out Ohio Stadium, but despite the lack of scoring, the game did live up to its usual hard-hitting reputation.

"It was probably, to this day, out of all the games I've ever played in, the hardest fought and hardest-hitting game I've ever played in, and that includes my career in the NFL," remembers Kenn, who went on to play for the Atlanta Falcons.

It was the second half, though, that burned a lasting memory in Kenn's mind.

"On our first possession of the second half, we went on a long drive and scored," Kenn says with conviction. "Then we kicked off. Ohio State moved it a little bit and punted it back to us at about the 25- or 30-yard line. We drove it right back down and scored.

"We kicked off back to Ohio State. They weren't successful, and they had to punt back to us. We went on another 75-yard drive, drove it down, and scored, and Bo went for two, and we got it. We were leading 22-0.

"After we got the 22-0 lead, we kicked off to them, and they couldn't move it, so they punted back to us. Well, we started to drive it, and we crossed over the 50-yard line, and there were probably less than six minutes left to play in the game, and all of a sudden Bo called a timeout from the sidelines."

Kenn was surprised by this move. He trotted over to the sideline with the rest of the offense confused.

"What the hell is he doing calling a timeout!" Kenn thought at the time.

Once he and the rest of the offense gathered around Coach Schembechler in front of the bench, the coach turned to them.

"First offense, you're done for the day," he commanded.

The second string entered the game, and Kenn walked to the bench at about the 50-yard line of Ohio Stadium, enjoying the satisfying moment of playing a dominant game.

"All of a sudden I realized, it was dead freaking quiet," Kenn recalls with a smile. "There were 87,000 fans in that stadium, and you couldn't hear a word.

"As I got to the sideline, I turned around and I looked across the field. There was Woody Hayes standing there, his arms crossed and that scowl on his face, and there wasn't a player or coach anywhere near him. I mean there wasn't anyone 10 yards from him, and I thought, 'Holy crap!'"

As Kenn watched Hayes brood at the sight of Michigan's second-string squad marching out on the field, the realization of what he and his teammates had done flooded over him.

"It's like you are so involved in the game or the contest as it's happening," Kenn explains, "that when you all of a sudden step back from it, you get to take in what's around you and what you've accomplished. You step back and say, 'Hey, we kicked their ass; we won the game.' It was just unbelievable. It was the greatest game I ever played in my life."

I was cursing—but it was happy cursing

It all happened against Notre Dame in 1991. Center Steve Everitt was having a great day, which was nothing unusual, but right before the half, the unexpected happened. Everitt had been blocking Bryan Young, the Irish nose guard, and mauling Notre Dame.

"I'm finishing blocks with my helmet flying off!" Everitt remembers, "I mean I'm finishing blocks with no helmet right in front of the student section, and they're going crazy."

Everything was going great until a smallish linebacker appeared from nowhere, got his helmet under Everitt's face-mask, and shattered Everitt's jaw. It happened on a play where Ricky Powers scored. Everitt didn't get in on the celebration. He was rolling around on the ground with blood coming out of his mouth.

The rest of the day was a bit of a blur. Everitt was removed immediately from the field by ambulance and taken to the hospital.

"They had to horse-collar my mom on the field," Everitt recalls. "I guess she was trying to run on the field when I was rolling around bloody. She actually jumped in the ambulance on the way to the hospital. She kept screaming at the ambulance attendants to give me an IV to sedate me. I guess I was going berserk.

"I was trying to tell everyone that I wanted to go back and play," he says with a smile. "I don't know whether that would have been very pretty, though."

That insistence to try to convince the ambulance attendants that his injury was nothing made his toughness legendary.

What happened in the hospital after Everitt arrived with the broken jaw only added to the lore. Despite being a bit out of it with painkillers and sedatives, Everitt knew that the Notre Dame game was still going on, and he was very interested in the outcome.

"I ended up watching Desmond [Howard] make 'The Catch,' on TV," Everitt says, "I saw that from the hospital with an IV in my arm. I ripped the IV out of my arm as we scored. I was cursing—but it was like, happy cursing."

And Everitt wasn't going to stay seated and out of action for very long if he could help it. He just told everybody he'd be back real soon. The problem was his jaw.

"It was like a bag of marbles," Everitt explains.

Doctors had to put three plates in his jaw to stabilize it. Unbelievably, he was back in 20 days, playing in the Wolverines' Big Ten opener against Iowa with a specially modified chinstrap on his helmet.

Coming back so soon after such a major injury is one of the reasons Everitt earned the reputation for his toughness.

"The jaw thing is probably when the toughness factor seemed to have peaked," he confesses. "But you know, I had a lot of injuries when I was here. Maybe I just had more chances to prove how tough I was, more than most people do. Half of it is luck. So I don't know whether I was that much tougher than anyone else. I just had a chance to show it more than most guys."

But that isn't the end to the story of Everitt's jaw.

"A year after the jaw was set, in my senior year," Steve begins with an embarrassed smile, "I was out at a restaurant with my parents. All of a sudden, my mouth started, like, gushing blood.

One of the screws in there had backed its way out, through my mouth.

"But there were actually two screws holding the plate in there, and only one of them was found. So, who knows where that other one is?" Everitt says with a malicious grin. "It's probably still floating around somewhere in my lower colon."

This is untouchable tradition

Center Steve Everitt's experience at Michigan as a football player and what he garnered as a person out of those four years is just as big a part of him as his tough reputation. As rough and tumble as Everitt is, when he talks about Michigan there is a respect and reverence.

"Everything about being here," Everitt explains, "I mean I played in the NFL for eight years, and there is not a team I played on after I left Michigan that even came close to my experience here. I mean I would have died on the field for this team. If I could have played 20 years for Michigan, I would have.

"Finishing up in my last game in the Rose Bowl with a win was a great way to go out. We were 4-0-1 against Ohio State while we were here, and that obviously is a highlight. I used to love to rub that in to guys from Ohio State who I played with or against in the NFL. That was always beautiful."

At a football players reunion in the summer of 2004, Everitt joined with his teammates and players from years past in Ann Arbor to rekindle those Michigan memories. The lasting effects of his days at Michigan were not lost on him as he spoke about the Michigan tradition.

"There are guys here I haven't seen in 10 years, and yet after seeing them for two seconds it's like we were just hanging out yesterday," Everitt explains. "There's just that unbreakable bond. I mean I've bled with these guys, and it's not like it doesn't happen at other schools, but it's just different here.

"Coming from where I came from down in Miami, I grew up a Miami Hurricane and Florida State fan. There is no histo-

Steve Everitt faces off against Notre Dame. They don't make 'em any tougher.

ry there. Here at Michigan, this is just untouchable tradition. To be a part of it and to be mentioned with guys that over the years you idolized, like Jumbo Elliott, to throw your name in the ring with those guys, well, that's just about enough to justify your existence."

We didn't have the chemistry

The 1984 team opened the year with a win over Miami, which at the time was ranked No. 1 in the country. The win vaulted Michigan to No. 3 in the land, but the next week, the University of Washington came to Ann Arbor and knocked off the Wolverines.

Michigan won their next two games and was ranked in the top 15, but then came game five of the season against Michigan State at Michigan Stadium.

The Wolverines were going with true freshman running back Jamie Morris because of an injury to starting tailback Rick Rogers. During the game, Morris slammed into the line on a running play and the ball popped free. In the ensuing race to recover the loose ball, quarterback Jim Harbaugh stretched his arm out to corral the bouncing pigskin, and a Spartan, diving to get to the ball himself, landed on the arm.

Harbaugh did not get up from the pile. His arm had been broken.

"That injury was really the start of our problems," captain Doug James recalls, "we had a lot of injuries. But to be honest with you, when I look back on that year, we were not the pro-totypical Michigan team.

"You know, Jimmy [Harbaugh] was the third-team quarter-back the year before, and when he got hurt, the guys who had to fill in for him had not been prepped for that. That wasn't their fault. We had injuries to our tailback, Rick Rogers, and our starting safety, Tony Gant, and as I look back on it all, I'll be honest with you, I just don't think we had the chemistry to over-come all the challenges we had to face."

That's a tough admission coming from a true Michigan man.

Mistaken identity?

The 1980 season had gotten off to a slow 1-2 start before the Wolverines reeled off win after win after win when they faced Purdue a week before they were to play Ohio State. It was a big game that was pivotal in the Big Ten race. A slipup by Michigan could take some of the luster off the battle with the Buckeyes, so the Wolverines went in ready to do battle.

George Lilja, All-American and co-captain, waged the war from center. At one point during the game, Lilja's jersey was nearly ripped off to the point where he couldn't go back out and play. On the sideline the equipment guys frantically scurried, searching through the big equipment trunks for Lilja's backup jersey. They pored through jersey after jersey, and they could not find it. Lilja stood there waiting as the next series went on without him.

Standing near the trunk was true freshman Doug James, who was oblivious to the frenzy going on by him because he was so engrossed in the game in which he knew he would not play. At that moment equipment manager Jon Falk looked up and noticed the benchwarmer. He walked right over to James, ripped the jersey over James's head and pads, and put it on Lilja.

"I am now standing on the bench in front of 105,000 fans at Michigan Stadium with no jersey on in just my shoulder pads and T-shirt," James chuckles. "The funny part of the story is I had a buddy of mine call me up later and say, 'I can't believe they put you in at center against Purdue in such a big game!' I told him I couldn't believe it, either."

The kicker: On the next play, with their real center in the game, Michigan drove down the field and scored.

We knocked their socks off

In 1983 head coach Bo Schembechler was in his 15th year at the helm of the Wolverines and was already considered legendary by many; at the same time George Perles was beginning to make his mark at Michigan State down the road in East Lansing.

During the recruiting season and eight months before the teams faced off, Coach Perles launched the first volley at his archrival in Ann Arbor to football writers when he said on national signing day that his recruits had "knocked the socks off" Michigan's class of players. That line made it to Ann Arbor and onto the bulletin board in the Michigan locker room.

"That comment from Perles really set the stage for the Michigan State game the next season," Doug James recalls. "So we went to East Lansing, and they had a good team. Carl Banks was a linebacker, Mark Ingram was a receiver, I mean they had a lot of great players.

"Bo, of course, had always given our pregame speech, but for this game, Jerry Hanlon [a longtime Schembechler assistant coach] just kind of took over the pregame talk. Jerry is always very emotional; he cries when he talks. So he got up in front of the team and he said, 'Don't let any son-of-a-gun think they can come in here and replace what this man,' and he pointed at Bo, 'has done at Michigan!'"

It was a message to the Michigan players that George Perles had not taken over the state, and to prove it all they had to do was win the game.

"We were all so pumped up, and I can't remember exactly what else Jerry said, but it was probably the best pregame speech I ever heard," James recalls. "We roared out of the locker room, and we beat Michigan State 42-0. And I swear, if we were still playing today, we'd be going in for another score right now!"

Run the ball!

O ne of the most accepted theories about winning football is really very simple. Most students of the game will tell you without hesitation that if you can run the football effectively on offense and stop the run on defense, you will have a great opportunity to win football games. Even in these days of pass-happy offenses, that theory will be repeated more often than not as being a solid recipe for success.

It was a theory that was adopted in 1995, because Michigan had a very strong offensive line that had played together all season and opened up a lot of room for ball carriers like Tim Biakabutuka. Over the course of the season, the Wolverines averaged more than 200 yards on the ground per game.

"We went into that Ohio State game, and they were ranked No. 2 in the country," offensive lineman Rod Payne recalls very clearly. "Our motto in the offensive line is very simple: run the ball, run the ball, run the ball. Sometimes, though, there is some give and take from coaches to players.

"We love our quarterbacks, but sometimes I think we may rely on them a little too much. In that game, we went out and opened up with a nice little drive. We were working them, and we felt as an offensive line that Ohio State was ready to give it up. We felt we had a real big game on our hands. But the coaches decided, in their infinite wisdom, to pass the ball. The pass got intercepted. We came off the field mumbling and grumbling to the coaches, 'C'mon, Coach, we can run the ball, let's stick with it.'"

The coaches apologized and agreed they would stay with the run. So the next series the Wolverines took the field and were moving it again. The ground game was working, but then, against the wishes of the offensive line, another pass was called. Incredibly, it turned into another interception. Again the offensive line grumbled at the coaches as the players headed back to the bench.

Although Biakabutuka had rushed for 197 yards in the first half, Michigan barely held a 10-9 lead. The offensive line figured they would stick with the strategy that worked in the second half.

But in the third quarter it happened again—the Wolverines had another good drive spoiled by an interception. At this point the offensive line had had enough.

"When we came off the field after that third interception," Payne says with conviction, "there was an attempted coup. It was a mutiny from the offensive line to the offensive line coach

Rod Payne, No. 52, paved the way when the staff listened.

to our coordinator, and to our head coach. We told all of them we were refusing to go back out there if we threw another pass! Believe me, it was a pretty heated conversation.

"To make a long story short, the coaches got the message. We went back out and rushed for more than 400 yards against Ohio State. It was the day Biakabutuka went for 313 yards on 37 carries. We beat the hell out of them!"

The final score was 31-23. Ohio State's hopes of a national title were ruined.

When the dust settled, Michigan had only thrown 18 passes, netted just 103 yards, and had three interceptions. The Wolverines ran it 58 times and outgained Ohio State in net yards, rushing 381 to 106. The offensive line clearly made the difference in this one.

Message received, loud and clear: Run the ball, run the ball, run the ball!

Get your hot dogs!

As the son of a former coach and player and the younger brother of a former Wolverine captain, Billy Dufek was in line for some good jobs on game days in Ann Arbor. After all, Jim Harbaugh, a son of a Michigan coach, was a ball boy during games at Michigan Stadium when he was a youngster. Well, Dufek got a similar assignment, but not nearly one as glamorous.

"I had a job as a kid through the sports information department, plugging in phones on the sidelines for the guy who called up to the press box and told them who made the tackle and who the ball carrier was," Dufek remembers.

Now that might not sound like much of a job, but for Dufek, the perks were what mattered.

"You see, that job gave me press box privileges, so at halftime, I could go up and bring back down 30 hot dogs to the field for all my buddies who were in the stands," he confesses. "They'd meet me at a spot, and I'd feed them all!"

Goose bumps

Billy Dufek became the third Dufek to wear the Maize and Blue when he walked out on the gridiron at Michigan Stadium as an offensive lineman. The feeling of being there is something he has never forgotten.

"I mean, how can you explain it?," Dufek marvels, echoing the sentiments of the players who have come and gone. "There are goose bumps going up and down your spine. It's the biggest stadium in college football. It is special. What can I say? I am very blessed to have played here, following my father and my brother and being a part of this great tradition.

"Playing at The Big House—there is nothing better."

CHAPTER SEVEN

Running Backs

This is it

In the early 1970s a smallish running back from Troy, Ohio, made the trip to Ann Arbor to see if Michigan was the place for him. His name is Gordon Bell, and his official recruiting visit coincided with the Michigan–Ohio State game, and the weather was typical of a Michigan November.

"When we drove up here for my visit," Bell says, "we experienced about four different kinds of weather. It snowed. It rained. It sleeted. And it hailed. And right before the Michigan team came out of the tunnel, they were using squeegees on the field because it was white from all the hail. So they got the field clean, and it was a beautiful green. I looked out over the campus from my seat up above the Stadium, and I thought to myself, 'I really like this place. I feel like I fit in.'"

But his mind wasn't fully made up. It took a sign from above, from football's Valhalla, to close the deal.

"Just as Michigan came out of the tunnel," Bell remembers, "the sun started to shine. It hit the gold pants. It hit the blue jerseys. All of a sudden, I realized, 'This is it!'"

I just left him there

The summer before running back Gordon Bell's senior year, he was at home in Ohio when he ran into some Michigan State players, including defensive back Tom Hannann, from time to time. The Spartan players had plenty to say to Bell about what would happen when the Wolverines and Bell came to East Lansing later in the year.

After that summer, Bell returned to Ann Arbor, and Michigan began the season with a win over Wisconsin and two ties against Stanford and Baylor and a true freshman quarterback, Rick Leach, at the helm. They turned to face MSU, and Bell remembered the words from the previous summer that the Spartan players had said.

The game was close throughout. Every snap of the ball had the potential to be a game-breaking play. The tension filled the stadium as the teams faced off in the fourth quarter—the score was tied.

During a Wolverine drive, the quarterback called for a sweep and pitched Bell the ball. He cut to the right-hand side of the line and came face to face with the talkative Hannann. Bell made another quick slant, turned the corner, and scored.

All Hannann could do was stand there and watch.

"As I got to the end zone, I remember laughing," Bell chuckles. "It was so funny that I just left him there after all the talking he had done over the summer. It was just great. I loved doing things against Michigan State, because they are such big talkers. They thought they had us, and we just took it away from them at that game."

By the way, the final score was Michigan 16, Michigan State 6.

It was surreal

We hear the statement many times from football commentators, coaches, and players that in big games, big-time players must step up and make big plays. Certainly in Michigan football history, there have been many who have stepped up in big games and made the difference. From the very beginning, whether it was Willie Heston, or Bennie Oosterbaan, or Tom Harmon, or Ron Kramer, or Anthony Carter, or Charles Woodson, there has always been a guy who has stepped up. They all worked within the team concept to create their own legend. They also seemed to play their best when the stakes were the highest.

Such is the case with Billy Taylor. Against Ohio State, Taylor was a running back who just would not be tackled. It wasn't that he didn't play well against everybody else; it was just that against the Buckeyes, Taylor made the plays that fans remembered the most.

In 1969, his sophomore year, he was hurt early in the season, and Glenn Doughty became the workhorse back for Michigan. By the end of the year, though, an injury to Doughty had given Taylor the opening, and he became the featured back. Taylor wound up being the team's leading rusher, averaging better than six yards a carry. Against an unbeaten and supposedly unbeatable Ohio State team that season, Taylor had his breakout game. A long tackle-breaking run in the first half really shook the Buckeyes, and it led to a Michigan score.

"They were pounding me," Taylor recalls, "I was working hard but just couldn't break a big one. Finally, when it came down to, you know, who's going to win this game? I was able to step up and break a big play. I still have a thorn in my side though to this day, that I didn't score on that play. I got bumped out of bounds inside the five."

It didn't matter that Taylor didn't score. A few moments later, fullback Garvie Craw crashed into the end zone, and Michigan was on its way to the upset of the century. The 24-12 Wolverine triumph over Ohio State, a team many considered one of the best college teams ever assembled, was heralded all over the country as one of the greatest victories ever.

For Taylor, the emotion of the victory was an out-of-body experience.

"I remember walking," Taylor says, "and my feet not really feeling the ground. It was the type of stuff that movies are made of and dreams are made of."

Taylor wasn't done with his heroics over Ohio State, though. Two years later in 1971, the Wolverines entered their game against the Buckeyes unbeaten and had already clinched the Big Ten championship. Taylor was completing his third straight year as Michigan's leading rusher. He had already passed the 1,000-yard mark, averaging better than five yards a carry on the eve of the Ohio State game.

Everything had changed since the 1969 contest. Michigan was the heavy favorite, and the game was a lot tighter. With about six minutes left, it appeared that Woody Hayes's Buckeyes would exact their revenge; Ohio State led 7-3 thanks to a long punt return for a score. Michigan got the ball back late, and it looked like the possession was the Wolverines' last chance.

With backup quarterback Larry Cipa at the helm, Michigan began a season-saving drive. There wasn't any panic. The Wolverines, predominantly a running team in 1971, stayed with the plan. A pass play was called here and there, but only to keep the Buckeyes honest. Slowly but surely, Michigan moved toward the winning score, and Taylor was waiting to plunge a dagger into the Buckeyes' hearts again.

With under three minutes to play, the Wolverines had moved inside the Ohio State 30.

"It was do or die. I remember praying as I went back to the huddle," Taylor recalls. "I kept asking God to please let me do something to make a difference here today.

"We actually had another play called, but Bo changed it. He called a wide sweep. And I remember after the snap, it was one

His motto was run north and south

Butch Woolfolk made a move he shouldn't have made against the Wisconsin Badgers in 1979.

And the result was a 92-yard scoring run that still stands in the Michigan record books as the longest scoring run from scrimmage.

"It was an off-tackle play to the left," Woolfolk remembers clearly. "I was following our lineman up to the left, and I cut back to the right. I probably should not have made that cut, though. Bo didn't like me doing all that cutting. Bo's motto was run north and south; 'Butch, run north and south.' But when I made that cut, there was an opening. When I got past the line-backers, it was just my speed that took me all the way. I remember running past our side of the field, and I knew it was over by then, because I had good speed. I just kind of enjoyed the last 50 yards running free."

Amazingly, two year later Butch went 89 yards for a score against Wisconsin in Madison. That run is ranked third all time in Michigan history. So in two carries against the Badgers, Woolfolk accounted for 187 yards. Way to follow the coach's advice.

Luck of the draw

Coach Bo Schembechler's luck in postseason play was dismal. Something always went wrong and caused the Wolverines to fall short. So when the team headed to the Rose Bowl to play the Washington Huskies in 1981, the Michigan fans were anxious. They wanted Coach Schembechler to get his first bowl win.

The Wolverines were leading 16-6 when they faced a third-and-long situation in their own territory. The fans held their breath, wondering if this was the tenuous point in the game

of those surreal situations. I mean everything worked. The ball was pitched to me perfectly. Then Cipa got the first block. Bo Rather got a crack-back block from his wide receiver spot. I remember following fullback Fritz Seyferth around the corner, and it was like again my feet weren't even touching the ground. When Fritz got the last block, I had one last guy to beat. He dove at me, and I leapt, stretched out, and he didn't even touch me. I knew I was gonna score, and when I crossed the goal line, I lost my breath.

"That was our last shot at it. If we didn't do it then, we weren't going to get it done that day. I remember raising my hands to the sky after I scored to thank God, and the fans started to engulf me. I couldn't even breathe. I never will forget that moment.

"I still have Bob Ufer's call of that play in the 'Favorites' on my computer at home, and it may be 30-odd years later, but I still get goose bumps listening to it."

The Wolverines won the game 10-7, and that play helped Michigan complete an undefeated regular season.

I remember it all, because I was the strong tackle on that play. I was one of the first guys to get to Taylor in the end zone to rescue him from the crowd. I don't know how much help I was, though. I remember being so happy I was beating Taylor on the helmet as much as the crowd was.

Nobody knew who I was!

In 1978, a running back named Harold Woolfolk thought he would never see the light of day in his first year. The New Jersey native was wrong. It wouldn't be long before Michigan fans forgot about the first name Harold and replaced it with the preferred name "Butch." It took a set of circumstances that coach Bo Schembechler didn't necessarily like.

"Believe it or not," Woolfolk remembers, "Harlan Huckleby got hurt, and Russell Davis got hurt. We really needed to bring up one of the freshman running backs, but Bo didn't want to do it. He wanted to red-shirt all of the freshman class.

Unfortunately for him but fortunately for me, he had to bring up Bubba Paris, and he had to bring me up, too. So there I was as a freshman, starting in Michigan Stadium.

"My name wasn't even in the program. Nobody knew who I was. Rick Leach had a great game that day, but we had to go to the running game, and I somehow managed to tweak out 140 yards and a couple of touchdowns.

"People were wondering, 'Who the hell is this guy?'"

That game he was also getting his first taste of Michigan Stadium and becoming a member of an historic tradition. Woolfolk had to experience it just like the Harmons and Kramers before him. And, like those before him, the moment was a bit overwhelming.

"It got to me when I went through the tunnel for the first time," Woolfolk recalls, "It was really, really, scary.

"Earlier in the season, I was sitting on the bench and I wasn't really part of the game, because as a freshman I knew I wasn't going to play. But when I got on the field as a starter, it was so scary.

"I mean I'm sitting in the I Formation, I'm back there dotting the 'I.' The fullback is in front of me, and Rick Leach is in front of him. I have to tell you, I couldn't hear anything! If Rick changed the play, I would have been lost. I just kind of moved when everybody else moved. That first game I played was, without a doubt, the most exciting game I ever played in Michigan Stadium.

"It was amazing, because I was so green. I didn't know what I was doing. I just followed Leach's lead and the older guys. They told me what to do. Every play, they would calm me down in the huddle. I was really scared about that game. I was really kind of numb about the whole thing.

"The real fear I had was messing up in front of Michigan Stadium. And the other fear was coming in as a freshman and trying to please Bo. I knew he didn't want to play me, and I knew if I made a mistake it would be worse."

Imagine all those thoughts running through your mind as an unknown 18-year-old in front of 100,000 people.

Butch Woolfolk, No. 24, didn't like people to call him Harold.

But Woolfolk survived the pressure. From that game on, Woolfolk was a regular in the Michigan lineup and a threat to pull off a spectacular play any time he touched the ball. Woolfolk led Michigan in rushing for three straight years, starting his sophomore season. Incredibly, he averaged better than five yards per carry over the course of those three years at a time when four yards a carry was considered excellent. Woolfolk still holds the record for the longest run from scrimmage by a Michigan player, and he was named the MVP of the 1981 Rose Bowl, Coach Schembechler's first postseason victory as Michigan's head coach.

where the tide would turn against them. The next call could make or break the game.

On the sideline, offensive coordinator Gary Moeller and Coach Schembechler were haranguing about what play to call.

"What do you want? What do you want?" the head coach asked quickly.

"Let's run the draw-pass," Coach Moeller replied. "Check with me."

(Given the yardage to go for the first down and the defense Washington probably would have used in that situation, it was more than likely the automatic called at the line of scrimmage by quarterback John Wangler would have been the draw play, but there was the chance that if Washington showed a different defensive scheme, Wangler could have tried a pass to Anthony Carter.)

Coach Schembechler looked at Coach Moeller.

"Aww, screw it, just run the draw!" he responded.

"We can't just run the draw," the offensive coordinator explained, pointing out the yardage needed for a first down.

But Coach Schembechler didn't want to argue anymore. The call was sent out to the players on the field.

"It was a bold call on Bo's part," running back Woolfolk recalls. "It was pretty amazing. We had like third and 24, and we had Anthony Carter split out wide. Of course the defense was looking at Anthony so they drop back immediately, and we called a draw play.

"When the play was called in the huddle, everybody was upset about it," Woolfolk chuckles. "I mean we had third and 24! What are we doing calling a draw?"

The offense went to the line and snapped the ball. The draw opened up the field, and Woolfolk slipped through the opening and made the first down.

"It was a great call," Coach Moeller admits. "We just wanted to gain a few yards and punt the ball back, and darned if Butch didn't bust it out of there for a first down."

With that first down, the drive continued, and disaster for the Wolverines was averted. With four minutes left in the game,

Stan Edwards scored the final touchdown to ice the victory for Michigan.

It was a huge win for the team. It wasn't a bad day for Woolfolk either, because he took home the MVP trophy. But in reality, the game was all about Coach Schembechler. He clearly deserved a bowl victory, and everyone on the team felt that way, including Woolfolk.

"It was an exciting win for him," Woolfolk remembers, "and really, nobody was thinking about the win for themselves, they were thinking about it as Bo's first bowl win.

"When we carried him off the field. It was just great. To this day, I think that is my No. 1 Michigan memory."

CHAPTER EIGHT

Receivers

Obviously, we fooled everybody

We have had the opportunity over the years to see some great receivers wear the Maize and Blue. Anthony Carter may be one of the most celebrated, but don't forget Desmond Howard, who won the Heisman. Michigan has always had a bunch of guys who have caught passes and made major contributions to their team's success. Every two or three years, a new one steps up to take over for the last one, and Michigan's offense sails ahead.

In 1985 Jon Kolesar came to Ann Arbor, but he didn't start making an impact immediately. As a freshman receiver, he didn't see the ball a lot from quarterback Jim Harbaugh until Kolesar spent the entire game against Illinois unguarded and ignored without a single catch to show for it. The next week before Michigan faced Purdue at home, Harbaugh was pestered by the coaches about not throwing to the lone receiver.

Apparently Harbaugh listened, because against Purdue, Harbaugh connected with Kolesar for a couple of touchdowns and 150 yards receiving. From that point on, Kolesar was a target Harbaugh could rely on for big catches.

Three weeks later, Harbaugh needed such a catch against archrival Ohio State in the waning minutes of the game.

The Wolverines had led 20-10 and looked as though they might take the easy win when a fourth-down pass hit All-America wideout Chris Carter in the end zone, and the Buckeyes were back in the game. On the ensuing kickoff, Michigan did not get a return, and they were stuck down in their own end. It was a tight spot. In order to protect their slim three-point lead, they needed first downs; they needed the clock to roll.

"The momentum had clearly changed," Kolesar recalls, "and on our first play after the kickoff, Bo sends fullback Gerald White up the middle for three yards. So everyone is getting all worried, because we're getting conservative. As a matter of fact, on the videotape of the game broadcast, the announcer talks about getting an up-close look at the hitting that's going on in the line of scrimmage. He thought, as a lot of people did, that Michigan was just going to grind it out, get a six-minute drive and put it on the ground to win it.

"Obviously we fooled everybody, including Ohio State. They thought we were going to run, too. They had everybody up close in the box. They actually had nine guys in the box. They had man-to-man coverage on me and [Paul] Jokisch, and they ran a safety blitz. The key to the play was Jim seeing the one-on-one coverage and having the confidence in me that he gained the previous couple of weeks. He stared down the safety blitz and put it up over the top for me."

Kolesar sprinted underneath the pass and ran away from Ohio State defender William White for a dramatic touchdown that closed the door on Ohio State and led to a 27-17 Michigan win.

Jon Kolesar gets a ride to the locker room after beating the Buckeyes. *Courtesy of Jon Kolesar*

Michigan Stadium was bedlam. For Kolesar, it was the first time the massive crowd at The Big House got his attention.

"As far as I'm concerned," Kolesar says with certainty, "after I scored with that pass, that was the loudest I've ever heard that stadium in my entire career. You know, Michigan Stadium, given all of its glory and size for some reason, doesn't resonate with noise. There are louder stadiums that carry less people. But on that day it was the loudest I've ever heard it. I've heard it louder since, but when I was a player, that was the loudest I can remember it ever getting."

We never think we're out of a game

In the 2003 and 2004 seasons, Michigan football had two of the greatest comeback victories in recent history. From certain defeat, the Wolverines were somehow able to gather them-

selves and put together heart-stopping, pressure-packed performances that snatched victory from the jaws of defeat.

Against Minnesota in 2003, the Wolverines trailed 14-0 at
half. In the third quarter they were still down 28-7. But
Michigan roared back with 31 points in the fourth quarter to
beat Minnesota 38-35. It was statistically the biggest comeback
in Michigan football history. It was, without question, a remarkable game.

But a year later against Michigan State, there was possibly
an even more dramatic comeback orchestrated by the
Wolverines. The Spartans had forged a 27-10 lead over
Michigan at Michigan Stadium with just 8:43 left to play. As at
Minnesota, this game looked to be over with the Spartans in
control. But Michigan got a field goal from Garret Rivas with
6:27 to play to make it a 27-13 game. On the ensuing kickoff,
Michigan's Brian Thompson made a heads-up play on an onside
kick and recovered the ball to keep it in the Wolverines' hands.
At that point, the momentum had completely changed sides.
Michigan looked like a different team.

In the huddle, the players fed off the shift and used it take
the game in their own hands. For wide receiver Braylon
Edwards, it was kind of like being back on the playground
where players draw plays in the dirt to explain everyone's role.

"We got the formation, then we said, you do this, you do
that, and Braylon, you go deep, we're going to throw it to you,"
Edwards admits. "And that's exactly what happened. [Chad]
Henne threw the ball up there, and we scored a touchdown. I
think it was called, 'Right-Strong, Braylon Go Deep.' That was
the play that was called."

Thanks to the aerial heroics of Edwards and the looseness of
the offense, the Wolverines were able to come back. The
Michigan wide receiver was unstoppable in the final eight minutes. He made two leaping catches while in hand-to-hand com-
bat with a Spartan defender to account for two touchdowns—
two scores that sent the game into overtime.

It wasn't until the third overtime that Edwards was able to
finish off the Spartans and clinch a thrilling 45-37 victory.
Edwards caught the game-winner streaking across the middle of

Braylon Edwards, No. 1, is also known as "The Playmaker."
Courtesy of Bill McKenna

the field, snatching a Henne pass out of the air and sprinting home from 24 yards on a critical third-and-nine play.

"We never think we're out of a game," Edwards says in a serious tone. "It's the way we play. After the Minnesota game last year and being in the Michigan State situation this year, we knew there was hope. All we needed was a big play, and we knew once we got the ball back, we had to make a big play. I told the coaches I was ready to make that play."

For the game, Edwards caught 11 passes for 189 yards and three scores. He was the player of the game.

"I felt great to be a part of that win," Edwards concludes. "I felt I had a helping hand in it. To be a part of a win like that in Michigan Stadium, I don't think the fans or players will ever forget it."

He should have thrown it to him

M ichigan looked like it was on its way to postseason paradise in the 1998 Hall of Fame Bowl against Alabama. In the third quarter the Wolverines had a 21-3 lead and seemed to be in control of the game. The ground attack by Jamie Morris racked up 234 yards on 23 carries, a Hall of Fame Bowl and Michigan bowl game record.

Then the Crimson Tide caught fire. They scored 21 unanswered points, pulling ahead 24-21, and a game that should have been a comfortable win for the Maize and Blue was now in danger of getting away.

With under a minute to play, Michigan was staked out on the Crimson Tide 20-yard line, facing fourth down and three yards to go. Quarterback Demetrius Brown was under center, and as the ball was snapped, he threw the game plan out of the window and decided to make a play.

"The read was to dump the ball off over the middle and get the first down," recalls coach Gary Moeller, who was running the team that day because coach Bo Schembechler was having heart surgery, with a laugh. "We had [Chris] Calloway wide open in there, but you never know, that crazy [Jon] Kolesar might have gone in there and told Demetrius to throw it to him."

Kolesar did no such thing.

"Demetrius should have thrown it to Calloway," Kolesar explains. "He was wide open over the middle, and I was well

Jon Kolesar, No. 40, celebrates his game-winning catch in the Hall of Fame Bowl. *Courtesy of Jon Kolesar*

covered. Alabama actually saw it coming. I lined up in the backfield on the play, and Alabama started shouting my name and number. They recognized it. We weren't fooling anybody. The only thing I told Demetrius, and I told him this after the Michigan State game when he threw six interceptions, was that if he threw it my way, I was either going to catch it or it was going to be incomplete."

Brown must have taken Kolesar seriously, because even though he was double-teamed, Brown lofted a jump ball into the corner of the end zone.

"When he threw it to me, I thought, 'Oh no!'" Kolesar remembers, "and that ball was in the air a long, long time. I was worried that I had been walled off by the Alabama defender so that I didn't have enough room to come down with the ball in bounds. When the pass came down, I leapt, and I saw the Alabama kid's arm wave in front of my face an instant before the ball hit me in the arms. It was a matter of centimeters, or he would have knocked that ball away. And when I came down, I had just enough room to get one foot in bounds. It's a game of inches, isn't it?"

It was the last of six passes the Wolverines completed in that game—but it made all the difference. The catch secured the 28-24 Michigan win, even if it was only by inches.

I'm getting the hell out of here

In football, injuries are a part of the game, and although players condition and equip themselves to avoid getting hurt, they understand that it is always a possibility. But most expect to be safe from harm once the game is over!

But after the 1979 Indiana–Michigan game, Wolverine tight end Craig Dunaway learned that celebrations could be just as painful as tackles as he headed to the locker room.

"As a freshman, I didn't play in the game," Dunaway explains. "But I'm watching, and I'm into it, and when Anthony [Carter] scored [on a prayer from John Wangler] and the ref's hands went up, you know we were jumping up and down on the sidelines. Everybody runs to the end zone and piles on AC. Personally, I don't know how he didn't get hurt.

"Well, I was in the pile somewhere, too, and as we un-piled, I remember everybody wanted to run to the locker room."

As the team headed for the locker room, they mingled with the mass of fans wanting to join them in the post-victory celebration. With his chinstrap unbuckled on one side, Dunaway ran toward the exit. All of the sudden his head was jerked back violently.

"Somebody had grabbed my chinstrap!" Dunaway explains. "It really spun my head around."

The chinstrap snapped off, and the anonymous fan ran away with his souvenir. Dunaway turned to chase him but then stopped.

"The hell with that, I'm getting the hell out of here!" he said as he turned back toward the tunnel before anyone else in the crowd decided to rip something else off.

A different standard

"October 4, 1975," the chalkboard read. Those words, written in 1979, have stayed with tight end Craig Dunaway, because they made him realize how high the expectations were surrounding those on the Michigan football team.

"I had only been on campus a month," Dunaway explains, "we'd had two games. We trounced Northwestern, and we lost to Notre Dame 12-10 on a blocked field goal. So, early the next week, we were in the full team meeting room getting ready for our third game against Kansas. [Coach] Bo [Schembechler] came into the room to start the meeting, and the first thing he did was walk to the blackboard and wrote a date down. It was 'October 4, 1975.'"

Everyone in the room sat in silence, wondering what the significance was of a date that was four years old. Then players started whispering to each other after someone realized what it meant.

"It was the last date that Michigan had been ranked outside the top 10 up until that day in 1979," Dunaway confesses. "We had gone from October 1975 to mid-September 1979 without ever falling out of the top 10 until that week after the loss to Notre Dame. That's when I realized wow, there is a degree of excellence expected here that is part of this program that I never realized until that moment. There is a different standard here!"

Craig Dunaway learned quickly about expectations at Michigan.

I was jacked out of my mind

One of the fascinating things about Michigan football is the emotion these players experience when they first come to play at Michigan Stadium. The effect of the experience at Michigan spans generations, and ironically they all describe similar feelings.

"I was jacked up out of my mind," wide receiver Braylon Edwards admits. "I had never been in a situation like that. There was so much anxiety, and so much was ready to burst out of me, it was like I was walking on air. I thought I was going to jump over the banner. It's just a great feeling to be a part of all that."

Tai Streets was one of Michigan's big play receivers in the national championship year of 1997. As a matter of fact, Streets caught two long passes in the Rose Bowl from Brian Griese that made a big difference in the Wolverine victory over Washington State. Streets has been out of Michigan for a while. He's had a nice career in the NFL, but even that can't match what Michigan provided him when he arrived in Ann Arbor from Illinois as a freshman in 1995.

"The first year I got there," Streets recalls, "we went into the Stadium at night when it was empty. It was a couple nights before our first game. It was amazing. I got that feeling, it was just incredible, and I don't know how to describe it. That was the greatest experience of my life, including playing in the pros and getting paid. There's nothing like my four years at Michigan. Running out of that tunnel and touching the banner, hearing that crowd roar, there isn't anything better! It's the greatest place you could ever play!"

Tight end Craig Dunaway played on the Wolverine teams of the early 1980s. As a native Pennsylvanian, he had nothing to which he could compare the Michigan Stadium experience.

"When I came out of that tunnel and looked at that sea of people, it was just unbelievable," Dunaway says with wonder. "It gives you goose bumps. I remember before almost every game at Michigan Stadium as the crowd was filling in during the last bit of warmups, I would get out of breath. It was as if I was hyperventilating. The adrenaline was pumpin', the butterflies were in my stomach, I was sweating profusely, and I wondered whether I was out of it or something! That never happened on the road. It didn't happen when I went to the Steelers and played at Three Rivers Stadium or wherever we'd go on the road in the NFL. There was just something about Michigan Stadium that made you get ready for a game in a different way."

We know. It is hallowed ground. It isn't like any other place.

CHAPTER NINE

Quarterbacks

We were the better team

In 1973 everything seemed to be all tied up. In the season finale, Michigan and Ohio State battled each other to a 10-10 score. The tie gave both teams identical records and both teams a share of the Big Ten title.

But there was going to be no tie for the Rose Bowl bid. One team would be chosen that following morning. Most people expected coach Bo Schembechler's Wolverines to get the nod because they had been favored at the beginning of the season, and the Buckeyes had been to the Rose Bowl the year before.

The shocker came that Sunday.

After the game, a hasty call to the conference athletic directors was made, a vote was taken, and Ohio State was declared the Big Ten representative for the Rose Bowl. To this very day, Coach Schembechler remains bitter about the vote.

One of the major reasons for the vote given by some Big Ten conference athletic directors was because of an injury suffered by Michigan quarterback Dennis Franklin during the game. Franklin had broken his collarbone, and his availability to play in the Rose Bowl was unknown at the time, but the athletic directors assumed that Franklin would be unable to play.

"I remember after I got hurt in the game," Franklin recalls, "I was led off the field by Dr. [Gerry] O'Connor. When we got to the locker room, O'Connor started playing around with my collarbone. At one point he started mashing down on it, and it went back into place. I'll tell you, I never felt such pain in my life. I thought I was dying. I wanted to scream. You could actually hear the bone slide back into place. It was horrible. But O'Connor had set it, and from that point on, it didn't really hurt.

"I knew I was going to have some rehab time, but I remember at that moment I felt like it was not going to be that difficult to play in the Rose Bowl in a little over a month. I didn't even think that we *wouldn't* be going to the Rose Bowl. Even though the game was a 10-10 tie, we were clearly the better team. The *last thing* I thought about was *not* going to the bowl.

"The thing that bothers me is that they never really gave me an opportunity to demonstrate that I would be well by the time the Rose Bowl came. It was crazy! It was very disappointing."

For Franklin and his teammates it had further repercussions than just the Rose Bowl bid. By being denied the Rose Bowl, the unbeaten and once-tied 1973 team could not go to any bowl because of the conference's rule prohibiting any other team but the Big Ten champion from participating in postseason play. It was an injustice. Coach Schembechler fought for years to get the outdated rule changed. In 1975 he got the change so other teams from the conference could go to bowls. It was too late, though, for Franklin and his teammates.

"And to this day, the thing that hurts the most is that there are so many memories other Michigan teams have had at bowl games that I've never experienced. None of the guys who came

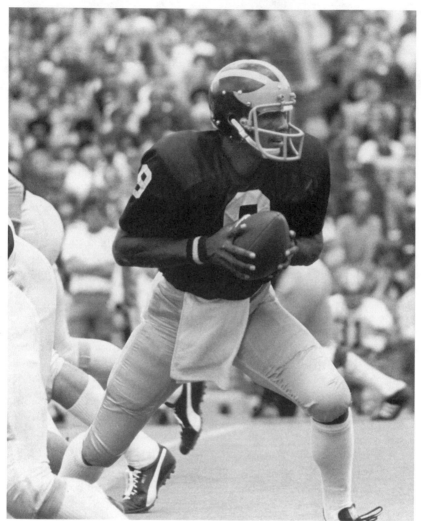

Dennis Franklin, No. 9, had 30 wins, two losses, and one tie as a starter, but never played in a bowl game.

to Michigan in my class got to go to a bowl. Not to the Rose Bowl, 'The Granddaddy of Them All,' or any other bowl. It's just so unfair."

Franklin's teams finished with a three-year record of 30-2-1. Those teams never played in a bowl game anywhere. It still bothers Denny Franklin. It still bothers his teammates. It still bothers Coach Schembechler. Hopefully, it still bothers those who voted to send Ohio State.

I'm the last to rush for 100

Did you know that Rick Leach, one of the best option quarterbacks Michigan has ever produced, only had one day when he rushed for more than 100 yards?

Did you know that despite Leach only rushing once for 100 yards, he is still the Wolverines' all-time leading quarterback in rushing yards?

Did you know that Steve Smith leads Michigan quarterbacks in the number of 100-yard rushing games with four?

Did you know that two times in Michigan history three players have rushed for 100 yards or better in a single game, and none of those players was a quarterback?

Did you know the last Michigan quarterback to rush for 100 yards or more in a game was Michael Taylor all the way back in 1987?

Taylor, who duked it out with Demetrius Brown for the quarterback position every year he was in school, was a very good option quarterback. He didn't have a strong arm, but he was smart in his student-like approach to the game.

"My first start was against Northwestern," Taylor says, "and I was just so anxious to show people what I could do, I didn't really notice the crowd. I typically tried to focus on what the game plan was and how to attack the defense. There's no question, that first game was special. I think I'm the last quarterback to rush for 100 yards in a game."

Taylor doesn't hold a lot of Michigan passing records, but the numbers still played an important role in his most memorable experience at the helm of the offense.

"We had lost to [Michigan State] the previous year when Demetrius threw those six interceptions," Taylor says unhappily, "but the next year, Bo made it an issue that if I threw six interceptions, he was going to come out and pull me off the field himself! The one thing he kept telling me was that if I took good care of the football, we'd have a great chance to win. That's really all I tried to do. We won that game, and it was a big victory for us. It gave us the confidence that if we could beat the defending champions, we could beat anybody.

"My main focus was winning football games. If we won, I was happy. If we lost, I wasn't too happy. To be able to win and play on the kind of teams that I played on here at Michigan is something else!"

I was petrified

D ennis Franklin began his run of 31 starts as the Michigan quarterback in his sophomore year of 1972 against Northwestern.

"We ended up winning that game 7-0," Franklin recalls, "but the thing I remember the most was how petrified I was coming through that tunnel for the first time. There were all those people in there. And in those days, it was before they started selling out every game! We'd have 80,000 or 85,000 in there. That was still a lot of people.

"In fact, the second game of the season they'd have band day. It was one of Don Canham's great promotions. He'd have all the bands from the local high schools in the area come in, and it would fill up the stadium. More importantly, it got more people to come and experience what a Michigan game was like."

Dennis was from Massillon, Ohio, which is a hotbed of quality high school football. They had drawn pretty good sized crowds for high school games, but Michigan Stadium was another animal all together. Franklin was overcome.

"I was never so scared," Franklin says with a smile. "I was just intimidated. I could not relax and, you know, be myself. I remember that more than anything about that first game. And late in that game, in the fourth quarter, I threw a touchdown pass to Bo Rather, a curl pattern, and we won 7-0. Michigan Stadium and a huge crowd, it's something that only a few of us have been able to experience, and it is a great experience."

A team, team guy

"Did you think Tom Brady was this good?"

It's a question I have been asked countless times by Michigan and pro football fans. Having broadcast all of Brady's Michigan games and having experience in the NFL broadcast booth, I'll tell you the honest truth. I thought Tom Brady was good enough to play on Sundays. I thought he was better than a sixth-round pick in the draft. But I'd be lying if I told you I thought he was going to have the kind of success he's had with New England. Three Super Bowl titles, two Super Bowl MVPs, and what many people think is an automatic pass into the NFL Hall of Fame were possibly unimaginable—even for Tom Brady.

Brady proved how tough he was in a game in his junior year against Ohio State in Columbus. It was a mauling, but the toughness and courage of Brady was absolutely unbelievable. Ohio State built a lead, forced Michigan into a passing game, and then blitzed the daylights out of him. He went back to pass 56 times! He was hammered and knocked down hard on about every snap.

But he kept getting up. He kept fighting.

He was a wreck after that game, but he never took a down off. He never asked for any help.

Some of the guys who played said that Brady was the guy keeping everybody else up. He was getting clobbered, yet he never lost sight of his responsibility to lead by example. A lot of guys saw something special in him during that test in Columbus.

As far as his quarterbacking skills, Brady can do just about anything you ask. His arm is stronger than you think. He is smart. He is very accurate. He gets even better when the play is more important. He prepares like crazy. And he has an uncanny calmness about him. I think of the poem "If" by Rudyard Kipling when I try and describe Brady's calm—"If you can keep your head when all about you are losing theirs and blaming it on you"—that's Tom Brady.

The truth is it is the intangibles that make Brady what he has become in the game of football. All of the tangibles are there, but the intangibles are the difference maker. One of his good friends is current Wolverine quarterbacks coach Scott Loeffler. He worked with Brady when Brady was learning his craft at Michigan. Coach Loeffler has better insight into Brady's capabilities than most, and when Coach Loeffler talks about Brady and his success, he never dwells on his physical skills.

"I think during his fourth year when he won the championship," Coach Loeffler says, "and he came back for his fifth year, you've got to understand, he came back to a situation where he was *fighting for his job from day one.* You're talking about a guy who just won the Big Ten title, won 10 games, and the first game of the next year he was *fighting for his job!* He handled that as well as anyone could.

"I'll never forget the Notre Dame game of his fifth year. We were at home. Tom started out the game real well. And then Drew Henson was put into the game, and there was a standing ovation for Henson in Michigan Stadium. When Tom was put back in the game, he led our team down for a score to beat Notre Dame 26-22. You knew there was something special about the guy.

"You want to talk about mental toughness? Here's a guy who just won the Big Ten championship, and yet everyone seemingly wanted Drew Henson to have his job, and they weren't quiet about it. Think about this: Against Syracuse in his last year, Brady gets pulled in the first quarter. Henson comes in and does a great job. We win the game, and Brady, *as a captain of the team,* addresses them after the game and sings 'The Victors' like nothing has happened. He was a team, team guy. And it doesn't shock me one bit that he's winning all these Super Bowls."

I think we saw all of this when Tom Brady was at Michigan—we just never realized how good he was.

The record doesn't lie. In the two years he was a starter, he led the team to 10 wins each season. He won a Big Ten title. He won an Orange Bowl game where he set Michigan and Orange Bowl records with a 34 of 46 passing night for 369 yards and

Tom Brady, No. 10, was as good as it gets. *Courtesy of John Gilman*

four touchdowns. He holds the Michigan record for most attempts in a game and most completions in a game. He is eighth all time in starts at quarterback with 25. Two of the top four passing yardage games in Michigan history have his name on them. He completed better than 60 percent of his passes both years he started. He was an Academic All-Big Ten performer. But most importantly, he was voted captain and the team's Most Valuable Player in 1999. Both of those honors come on a vote of your teammates.

Next time I'm asked if I knew how good Tom Brady was when he was at Michigan, I'm going to say, "No, but I should have."

He did exactly the same thing at Michigan that he's doing in the pros.

I *watched* it all, I just didn't *see* it.

CHAPTER TEN

Defensive Line

All about the team

Tom Goss played football at Michigan in the mid-1960s. He was a solid defensive lineman who anchored some pretty good defenses for Bump Elliott. Goss's memories from his playing days revolve around his teammates and their rather interesting physical traits.

"The guys I played with are what I remember most," says Goss, who went on to become Michigan's athletic director, "having Phil Seymour playing to the left of me weighing about 120 pounds. He was so thin, and he still is; he may weigh 130 now. And Cecil Pryor used to line up behind me, and he had nothing but bird legs. He had the thinnest ankles in history, but they could both play."

For Goss, his teammates and the team are always central to what he remembers about his time at Michigan Stadium.

"My senior year, we had the great Ron Johnson," Goss begins, "and he broke all kinds of records in the Wisconsin game in 1968. As a defense, we held Wisconsin down, and that was one of my better games individually, and one that I will always remember. I also remember when we played Michigan State that year down here in Ann Arbor, and we beat them 28-14. That game was special because they had beaten us the year before."

Where's my arm?

Defensive lineman Tom Goss remembers well the arm pads he wore on his forearms. They had his number stenciled on them. They weren't anything fancy, but they stick in his mind because of a game at Minnesota his junior year.

During a Minnesota drive, Goss lined up to face the offensive line. After the snap, two lineman attacked him. One of them—John Williams—grabbed Goss by the arm. He jerked down on Goss's arm and the pad at the same time Goss pulled up on the arm. Pop!

Goss landed flat on his back and noticed that linebacker Frank Nunley was knocked out on the play.

Then he noticed something else. He couldn't feel his forearm.

The trainers scrambled around him. Goss looked directly at them.

"Where is my arm?" he asked concerned.

He looked and saw his elbow laying off to the side and realized it was numb.

"My elbow was actually pulled out of the socket, and that was the most painful experience in my life," Goss explains. "I went to the sideline, the trainers popped it back in, they gave me two painkillers, and that was that. That's when men were *tough*."

Goss did not go back into the Minnesota game that day, but two weeks later he did play against Ohio State with his arm and elbow taped to his side.

Can you imagine? First of all, that he was able to play two weeks later and second, that he was able to be effective as a defensive lineman basically playing one handed!

Generation after generation

At Michigan it seems that the act of being a Wolverine on the field automatically bonds you to other Wolverine players no matter when they played. The Big House with its tradition and glory unites them in a way that cannot be explained.

"You know, when you see these guys who played years ago," defensive lineman Grant Bowman observes, "you get to see how excited they get to see somebody who has been playing and just been through it like I have. For me, it's neat to see all these people who have been through similar experiences. We have a sort of kinship. Even though you've never met some of them, the first time you shake their hand, you know there is something similar between you."

These men all ran through the tunnel at Michigan Stadium, heard the crowd roar as they walked onto the field, sang "The Victors" with unbridled fervor, and lived and died with the Maize and Blue. Every player—whether playing in 1962 or 2002—has a moment like that that stays with them forever.

"I'll never forget the first time I ran out of the tunnel and touched the ['Go Blue Go'] banner against Notre Dame," Bowman says proudly. "It was our freshman year, and we came back late behind Tom Brady and got a touchdown to win."

I helped turn the tide

After losing to Ohio State in his sophomore and junior seasons, defensive lineman Grant Bowman, who is from a town in Ohio near Columbus called Blacklick, had a burning desire the get a victory against the Buckeyes. He knew it wouldn't be easy. Ohio State came into Michigan Stadium in 2003 ranked No. 4 in the country; Michigan was ranked No. 5.

Grant Bowman, No. 60, was not very big, but his heart was.
Courtesy of Bill McKenna

Michigan needed the win to get to the Rose Bowl and to secure the outright Big Ten title. It was a huge game.

"I always wanted to make plays," Bowman says with conviction, "that would help turn the tide of a game. One play I am especially proud of came in my last game against Ohio State in Michigan Stadium. In the fourth quarter when they were driving, I got a sack on third down to force a punt. It just felt so good because it was the biggest game I played in. It was the biggest thing I've done."

Bowman wasn't the biggest defensive lineman Michigan has ever had. He wasn't the fastest. All he did was make plays; he was as big as they come in that department.

I remember that vividly

In the mid-1960s Michigan had a great defensive tackle named Bill Yearby. Yearby was known for his fierce play. But one time against Northwestern, his ferocity on the field was displayed before the ball was snapped.

A Northwestern offensive lineman didn't wait for the play to begin. He jumped offsides—intentionally—and smacked Yearby. Yearby, a two-time All-American and voted by the team as the Most Valuable Player in 1965, was not going to let that player get away with the unfair hit. He was pumped up, and he exploded.

"I know what I should have done, but at the same time, I was fired up to get the game going," Yearby confesses nearly 40 years later. "It was kind of funny afterward. I think it kind of got everybody hyped up. In truth, I was glad I did it."

It was a good thing the ref stepped in and calmed things down, because as captain and fellow linemate Jim Conley suggested, Northwestern was trying to get Yearby off his game and maybe even out of the game. He was such a dominant player that the Wildcats felt they needed to target him to have a chance to beat the Wolverines.

What a beautiful-looking sky

Defensive linemen generally enjoy chasing quarterbacks—especially when it is behind the line of scrimmage. But in the early 1960s, Navy had a quarterback named Roger Staubach who took all of the fun out of pursuing the man at the helm. His scrambling style of play made lining up against him a nightmare.

One Saturday in Ann Arbor sophomore defensive lineman Bill Yearby had spent most of the afternoon chasing Staubach and trying to contain the constantly moving Midshipman.

"He was a great quarterback," Yearby recalls with a smile. "I was young. I had a lot of energy that day, and I was always on him, chasing him around. Well, right before halftime, they ran an off-tackle play...."

The eager defensive lineman charged forward. Smack!

Yearby was flat on his back, looking up at the heavens. It was a hot, sunny day.

"What a beautiful-looking sky, you know!" Yearby thought, drawn into the deep blue above him. "Wow! What a beautiful day!"

All of a sudden a man came into the picture. He waved his hand in front of Yearby's face.

"What's your name?" he asked the stunned lineman.

Yearby looked at him blankly.

"Who are you?" Yearby responded.

The trainer explained what had happened.

"I was knocked out cold," Yearby says through his heavy laugh. "I didn't remember anything. But when I came to, I was looking at the sky and it was the most beautiful thing I had ever seen. I will never, ever forget that."

Part of the tradition

Bill Yearby came into the program in the early 1960s with a group of guys who were just as committed as he was to making Michigan football a program people were attracted to with a tradition the school could embrace. They played for Bump Elliott, and as Yearby says, it wasn't all about wins and losses.

"It was a tremendous time as far as I'm concerned," Yearby says with pride, "because we were about building a program up here. I think we were successful at it, too.

"As I watch the teams now, it's just amazing. I always feel a part of it. It's always exciting. I mean, I never will forget Ron Kramer and Jim Pace and all of those guys who played up here. As a kid, I used to watch those guys. I never thought that I

tore his helmet off, and threw it with all of his might.
hrough the sky and landed on top of the football

e entire practice froze. Everything stopped," O'Neal
a grin. "I mean offensively and defensively, the coached. Bo [Schembechler] stopped. They couldn't believe
were in disbelief. So with practice stopped, equipment
Jon Falk had to go get a ladder and climb up on top of
ding to get my helmet back.
hink they were too much in a state of shock to say any-
me."

An obese lady broke her leg

well remembered among those who played football at
igan under Bo Schembechler that his penchant for
ness was legendary. I recall as a player in Coach
echler's first years in Ann Arbor that we never talked
astern Standard Time or Daylight Savings Time; no, we
referred to the time as BST, Bo Schembechler Time. It
ally 10 minutes ahead of the actual time. In other words,
ting was called at 10 a.m., Bo Schembechler Time was
m. If you remembered to stay on BST, you never found
running penalty miles or extra laps after practice.
e military precision with which Coach Schembechler
his itineraries when he took his teams on the road is
ing to admire. As a matter of fact, a great many of his
e still practiced today. When an itinerary for a road trip
e Michigan staff is made, it looks a little like this:

Team Meeting (Football Building)	2 p.m.
Buses Leave	2:30 p.m.
Arrive at Airport	3:05 p.m.
Plane Leaves	3:20 p.m.
Arrive at Chicago (O'Hare)	3:25p.m. (CST)
Bus to Stadium (Walkthrough)	3:50 p.m.

would get the opportunity to play at Michigan, and I can't tell
you how grateful I am that I did get a chance to play here.

"I came from the east side of Detroit, and we played at
Mack Park on Fairfax and Mack, and we might have had 200 or
300 fans there for high school games. To come up here, and
walk in that stadium and see all those people, it was amazing. It
was a total culture shock, because I had never been in an environment like that.

"When I came here as a high school kid to watch a game, I
never thought that I could be a part of it, but I wanted to be. So
that's what I set my sights on."

For Yearby, Michigan means so much more than football. In
many ways, the Wolverine football experience molds a person
beyond the Xs and Os of the game.

"You know, football only lasted so long," Yearby explains.
"What I really appreciated was the life experience I received
here."

We appreciated all you did, too.

I better wake up and start playing

For Timmy Davis, a Wolverine middle guard in the early
1970s, the first impression The Big House made was all
about the people in the stands.

"It was my sophomore year," Davis remembers, "and our
middle guard, Donny Warner, got hurt. I had to go out there
and fill in for him, and it was the first opportunity that I had to
play. I think I was out there for four or five reps, and the only
thing I was amazed at was the crowd. It was so overwhelming. I
remember from that point, after I got knocked in the head a
couple of times, that I better wake up and start playing football,
or I would *be* one of those fans sitting in that crowd."

Although Davis remembers that first moment when he got
into a game vividly, he says that the more he played, the more
surreal it all became. As he played more and the games became
more important and the nose guard was in there at crunch time,
his senses seemed to elevate with the intensity of the contest.

"I think more or less, I was in a dream more than anything else," explains Davis, who never garnered a win against Ohio State but had 21 tackles against the Buckeyes his junior year. "When I would run out there, I would just see the wave of people. I could not believe that this many people were watching me and the football team that I played for. It was really like a dream, and I can't tell you how glad I was that I was with Michigan."

CHAPTER E

Linebac

It is
Mic
promp
Schem
about
always
was us
if a me
9:50 a.
yourse

Everything sto

During preseason practice, lineba
his fellow inside and outside l
intensely to prepare for the upcomin
coach Bill McCartney watched, one a
through the motions of the drill. Whe
take a shot, he was knocked down hard
could get up, another player fell on his
le. O'Neal writhed on the grass in pain
But that didn't stop Coach McCart
right over where O'Neal was bunched
O'Neal watched the feet and legs of
they almost trounced him and became

the tur
It cut
buildin
"T
says wi
es stop
it. The
manage
the bui
"I
thing t

Leave Stadium for Hotel	*4 p.m.*
Arrive at Hotel	*4:20 p.m.*
Dinner	*5:30 p.m.*
Movie	*7 p.m.*
In Room	*9:30 p.m.*
Lights Out	*10 p.m.*

That would be a sample itinerary for a Friday of a road trip to Northwestern. This minute-by-minute schedule planning hasn't changed much in more than 35 years, and a player never dared to be late to anything. Heck, I can remember Coach Schembechler chewing out one of the airline guys when the plane was late picking the team up because of bad weather. He wasn't kidding, either. If you were late, it didn't matter who you were, you would have to pay sooner or later.

Such is the case with linebacker Calvin O'Neal on a trip to Wisconsin one year.

"It was me and a couple of other guys," O'Neal recalls with a smile. "After we arrived, we checked in, got all our stuff into our rooms, then we kind of laid around for a little while. Normally, you get the time for the meal on the itinerary, but on this trip I don't remember getting the time. Anyway, after a few minutes we started for the elevator to get to the banquet room for the meal.

"When we got to the room where the meal was being served, we heard all the dishes clanging and banging and everybody was sitting down eating. It was clear that they had been eating for a while! I thought, 'Oh my goodness!' The worst thing you could do with Bo, as you know, was be late. Well, forget it. We thought it was the end of the world.

"Gary Moeller saw us standing out in the hall, so he hurried out and got us.

"He whispered, 'Just come on in and sit down, and be quiet.'

"So we did, but we knew it wasn't over. We knew we were in trouble. We all decided we had to come up with a story to get out of this thing. So we came up with a story.

Calvin O'Neal, No. 96, was a much better linebacker than storyteller.

"Our story was while we were on the elevator going to dinner, this obese lady fell in the elevator and broke her leg. We had to call 911 and when they came, we had to help get her out of the elevator. That was the story we gave Bo."

Surprisingly after the guys told that whopper, Coach Schembechler did nothing—right then.

"Bo told us he'd deal with it at the team meeting on Sunday," O'Neal says.

The Wolverines, with O'Neal and his tardy buddies in the lineup, went on to win the game in Camp Randall Stadium that Saturday afternoon, but O'Neal and friends knew the weekend wasn't over.

After an uneventful return trip from Madison and a Saturday night at home in Ann Arbor, the team returned to the football building on Sunday for the usual postmortem on the victory over the Badgers. In these postmortems, there is the normal full team meeting first, and then the team breaks into offense and defense. Game film is then replayed with coaches correcting mistakes that were made and praising the good plays that were made. After this particular game, Coach Schembechler changed the normal schedule. Instead of going over the Wisconsin game, then splitting into offense and defense, the first thing he did was single out O'Neal and call him to the front of the room.

"Believe me, this is a true story," O'Neal laughs. "At the full team meeting, Bo called me up and said, [O'Neal drops his voice and growls, doing his best Coach Schembechler impression] 'O'Neal, get up here, and tell this team that cock-a-mamey story that you told me about why you were late for dinner in Wisconsin!'

"So I had to stand up there and tell them. The entire team died laughing throughout the entire story. I mean they were on the floor laughing."

Now you might think that ended the story. The shame of getting up in front of the entire team and telling that yarn wasn't enough punishment for O'Neal and friends.

"Needless to say," O'Neal concludes, "we ran extra every day after practice that season. Bo made us run."

What am I doing here?

It was a good time to be playing football in 1967. As linebacker Phil Seymour walked through the darkness of the tunnel at Michigan Stadium, he could hear the murmurings of the crowd as they waited for the team to emerge. The rumble started out light and then grew into a roar as the Wolverines rushed out of the tunnel and onto the field. In the background amidst the cheers, Seymour heard the band play and saw the stands packed with Michigan Maize and Blue and Michigan State green.

"Holy crap!" he said to himself. "What am I doing here?"

And that thought continued to echo in Seymour's head as he began playing for the Wolverines.

Seymour was by no means a standard linebacker. He was undersized for the position, weighing only 190 pounds. His tall and slender figure stood out against the bulkier frames of his fellow defensemen and opposing offensive linemen. He was not a prototypical football player, but he was twice named All-Big Ten and was as tough as nails to play against.

Against Duke before Seymour made the starting squad, the sophomore was placed on the kickoff team, and so he went out on the field to perform his assigned task. After the kickoff, he returned to the sideline to watch the game unfold. He particularly wanted to watch his mentor, middle linebacker Tom Stincic. Duke grinded out a drive that finally the Wolverine defense was able to stop. As the defense came off the field, Seymour saw Stincic step out from the group. He was covered in blood! His pants were stained red, and his face and arms were dripping a mixture of blood and sweat. Seymour was shocked.

"What am I doing here?" he asked himself out loud. "My mom didn't raise a fool. I better get outta here!"

But Seymour stayed despite the nagging thought that he just didn't belong. He played it out.

Later that season, Seymour, in his first Big Ten start, and his teammates faced the Minnesota Golden Gophers in Minneapolis. This matchup was a year after Michigan had handed the Gophers a sound beating 49-0, and Minnesota was not going to forget it—they had printed the score on their helmets for motivation.

"I was playing right next to Tom Goss in a new 4-3 defense we had installed that season," Seymour explains. "It was early in the game, maybe the first play of the game, and when it was over, I saw that Tom Goss had gotten hurt. His elbow was at a weird angle. It had been dislocated.

"The refs had stopped play to take Tom off the field, so we were back in our huddle when [fellow linebacker] Rocky Rosema stumbled in, looked at me, and asked, 'Where am I?'

"Now understand I'm weighing about 190 pounds, and I've just seen one of my guys get carried off, and another one is talking goofy. That's when I heard one of the Minnesota guys from across the line say, 'We got two of them on that play, let's get some more.'"

The same question that had riddled him the entire season popped into Seymour's mind.

"Later in that same game," Seymour chuckles, "They ran a sweep to my side of the field. I got double-teamed by Charley Sanders and John Williams. [Both of these players went on to the NFL and very distinguished careers.] Well, I spun out of the double team, maybe about 15 yards downfield. I mean, I was like a guy on roller skates at an ice rink. So I was standing around the pile when Sanders came up and blasted me from behind over the pile. It was embarrassing enough to get blown off the ball 15 yards, but now to get blasted twice."

The linebacker could hear the same voice in the back of his mind: "What are you doing here?"

Seymour came off of his sophomore season and developed into a solid linebacker. Over his next two seasons the question that had haunted him so often in the beginning of his Michigan gridiron career faded into the background. He now had experience, and he knew a few more tricks. He survived out on the tough turf of Big Ten football; that is until one Saturday during his senior year.

"We were beating Purdue pretty badly that day," Seymour recalls, "and I was playing against a guy named Donnie Green. He went on to a great pro career. Well, early in the game, I was rushing the passer, and I'd filled out to about 200 pounds, maybe. Well, Donnie Green hit me in the chest with his helmet, and it liked to kill me. I had to get him back for it, so later in the game, I was rushing the passer again, and I hit Green as hard as I could with the heel of my hand on the side of his helmet. On that play, the Purdue quarterback threw an interception. So I was running down the field to block for our guy, who intercepted the ball. I had forgotten about the shot I had given Green, but it must have affected him because he ran about 50 yards, and while I was standing next to the pile, Green ran right over the top of me from behind!

"At that moment, I again thought to myself, 'Why am I playing football?'"

Although Seymour clearly got knocked around a lot as an undersized linebacker, he may have been the toughest 190-pounder who ever wore the Maize and Blue winged helmet. Those who had to block him never wondered for a moment why he was out there. He was out there because he was good.

It was unbelievable to watch

In 1998, the year following the Wolverines winning the national championship, Michigan started off the season 0-2. They lost on the road at Notre Dame in the opener and then returned home and lost that debut to Syracuse. It was not the start anybody expected or wanted. It also happened to be the first year in Maize and Blue for a linebacker from New Jersey named Victor Hobson.

"There are a lot of memories that go through my mind," Hobson starts, "and when I was younger, I spent a lot of time on the sidelines. I got to watch a lot. And really, one of the most vivid memories I have is when Syracuse came to town, and Donovan McNabb pretty much had his way with our team.

"I mean he was shaking guys left and right. He was even losing people who were chasing him from behind! It was unbelievable to watch! As a freshman, I watched that and said, 'Wow!' Hopefully I can get to that point one day. I had never seen anybody have that kind of day against us. It was the first time I saw it, and it was the last time I saw it. Not too many people come into Michigan, at The Big House, our house, and have that kind of day."

That day was Hobson's first game in Michigan Stadium. It was his first run under the banner into a sold-out Big House.

"It was definitely impressive," Hobson says with a grin. "I mean when you run out there, you really don't know what to expect. There are hundreds of thousands of people looking down at you cheering, the adrenaline is flowing, and at first, you don't know how to react. In reality, it doesn't really hit you until after the game is over, and you think, wow, I just played in front of a lot of people!"

A late hit

Victor Hobson had distinguished himself as a very good linebacker since that first game as a freshman. Selected as a captain and named All-Big Ten in his senior year, Hobson had led his team to the Citrus Bowl against the Florida Gators.

The two teams put more than 900 yards of combined offense on the board against each other. The seesaw affair saw Michigan trail three times in the first half, but they came back each time to take a lead at the break. At the beginning of the third quarter, Florida again took the lead before the Wolverines took it back 28-23 midway into the third. This game though, came down to the bitter end, and it was Hobson who became the key player.

Hobson had performed brilliantly all day, recording a career-high 12 tackles. He had delivered a key sack late in the game that was instrumental in a Michigan field goal drive to make the Wolverine margin eight points at 38-30. But with the clock winding down, Florida had the ball. They were driving for a possible tying score. Hobson and the Michigan defense had been under pressure all day thanks to the play of the Gators' outstanding quarterback, Rex Grossman.

Then, the play that could have closed the game out for Michigan happened. Grossman was flushed out of the pocket, he threw wildly, the ball fell incomplete—it was over, a Michigan win.

No, wait.

A penalty flag was thrown on the play. It was a roughing the passer penalty on Michigan. Florida was still alive. The penalty was called on Hobson.

"You know," Hobson explains. "Everybody was trying to make that big play. When the quarterback scrambled to the sideline, I just wanted to make the big hit. That's always what I was looking to do. As I jumped to go hit him, he stepped out of bounds and I hit him anyway. I was hoping I wouldn't see a flag, but a bunch of flags hit me in the helmet."

Although Hobson knew he had made a huge mistake, he also knew as a leader of the team, he couldn't get despondent about it and forget the job still left to be done.

"While I'm on the field, I never doubt myself," he says. "I didn't get down on myself at all. The time to get upset at yourself is after the game if you don't recover from the mistake."

Well Hobson found quite a way to recover. On the very next play, Florida tried a trick play to catch Michigan by surprise. It was a wide receiver reverse pass that backfired. As the pass fluttered through the air, Hobson was there to intercept it and close out Florida's last hope.

"It came right to me," Hobson remembers. "I couldn't think about doing anything but running. I got about 20 yards, but I was so out of breath, I was *looking* for someone to tackle me.

"It was kind of a bad play-good play kind of thing. It evened itself out. I felt like a million bucks after that interception. I was also able to walk off the field in my last game at the University of Michigan a winner. It made me feel that much better."

They made this guy's life miserable

An integral part of Michigan football is the passing down of knowledge and technique from an older player to a younger player. It is a Michigan tradition, like "The Victors." A responsibility seems to fall on every upperclassman when he moves from his sophomore year to junior year, and once he moves up the ladder and becomes a senior, the importance of making sure this Michigan tradition is passed down becomes a part of you. As a senior, a player's legacy is not only judged on his team's performances, but on what he has left behind for those who follow.

Tom Stincic was a very tough, hard-boiled middle linebacker in the mid-1960s. He was good enough to be an All-Big Ten selection twice and went on to play professionally, where he played with Super Bowl champions. Make no mistake, he was a good one.

When I enrolled at Michigan, Stincic was a senior. As a freshman, I didn't compete against the varsity, and based on what I had heard through the grapevine about Stincic, that was just fine by me. The phrase being eaten up and spit out more often than not referred to Stincic's style of play. If you got in his way, you weren't there for long, and in the process you paid a price to venture near his area of responsibility.

But Stincic, who was known and revered by the linebackers who followed him, credits his style of play to some veterans who showed him the ropes when he first became a part of the team.

Before his first game as a starter against Oregon State, Stincic had heard about a receiver on the opposing team that was six foot eight and a basketball player. The wideout was huge and intimidating to the sophomore linebacker. Finally Stincic had made it to the big time, playing for Michigan, and his opponent had a giant on their side. As Stincic trotted out onto the field, he was a bit stunned at the prospect of playing against this kid.

But senior defensive backs John Rowser, Rick Volk, Mike Bass, and Dick Sygar were not. They had it in their minds that this receiver from Oregon State was *not* going to catch a pass. And they made sure he knew it.

On every play they let him have it, tattooing him with big hits and punching him in the face. They made this guy's life miserable that Saturday.

After every play they got back in the huddle. Stincic watched them.

"It's your turn," one of them said. "You hit him first this time, and I'll be right in there after you."

Stincic could not believe the ferocity with which these guys were playing.

"Oh my gosh, we're going to get in fights and they're going to get penalties," he thought to himself.

But he marveled at these men who were not going to let a player who happened to be taller dominate them on the gridiron. Stincic walked onto the field wide eyed that day with fear of his opponent and walked off of it wide eyed in awe of his teammates.

"Those defensive backs, along with linebacker Frank Nunley, taught me so much," Stincic recalls. "They had it in their minds that Oregon State was not gonna stop us, no matter what. It was just incredible that every game, even some that we weren't successful in winning, you'd see these guys reacting in the huddle to the good and the bad. Even in adversity, they taught me a lot. They were the guys I looked up to."

As he became a senior, Stincic provided that same kind of leadership to the younger guys on his teams. It is a formula that has proven very successful through the years and a great source of pride to all of those who have gone through the program.

"I think it's a little more impressive, the older I get," Stincic explains with a grin. "Now I watch Michigan on TV every week, and people say to me, 'Hey, they're pretty good!' I tell them when it was my turn, I took my shot and did my share. Now I see all that Michigan is and what it means to so many people over so many years, and it puts what I did in perspective.

"Hey, I've played in Super Bowls, and I've won Super Bowls, but still Michigan is pretty much the highlight."

Here is a human phenom

I n my humble opinion, the best defensive performance I've ever seen from a Michigan football team was against Auburn in the Sugar Bowl in January 1984. Michigan had finished second in the conference that season behind Illinois. They had lost by one point to Washington in Seattle during the non-conference schedule, and they had dropped a 10-point decision to the Illini in Champaign. They were a very good 9-2 team when they accepted a bid to the Sugar Bowl as the Big Ten's runnerup.

Auburn, on the other hand, was a team with designs on the national title. As a matter of fact, if the BCS rankings had been used in those days, Auburn would have played in the national title game. They had a defense that was fast and simply outstanding. But their defense didn't get very much publicity, because the Auburn offense featured a backfield of Bo Jackson, Lionel James, and Tommy Agee, who would all go on to play in the NFL. (Jackson, of course, became a Heisman Trophy winner and a household name, thanks to his exploits in football and Major League Baseball.) They ran the Wishbone, and no team had stopped them that season. The Auburn offense was a Mt. Everest to climb for the Michigan defense.

But Michigan held Auburn and those three exceptional backs scoreless in the first half. The only scoring the Wolverines gave up were field goals. Auburn kicked their third field goal of the second half with 19 seconds left to win it 9-7. Imagine an offense with Jackson, James, and Agee shut out from scoring a touchdown against an undermanned Michigan defense. Even in a loss, I still rank it as the best performance by a defense I've ever seen.

To be in the middle of that effort was one of the great memories linebacker Tom Hassel has of his days in Maize and Blue. He says the credit for that outstanding performance goes to the guys he played with and defensive coordinator Gary Moeller.

"Gary Moeller was the most creative guy I ever played for," Hassel says without hesitation. "He had a defense for every offense out there. That defense against Auburn was a variation of the Michigan defense, but if there were running backs out there named Bo Jackson, "Little Train" [Lionel James], and "Big Train" [Tommy Agee], Moeller made sure we had an answer for them. In that game, Moeller kept repeating to us, 'You guys *have* to get to the ball!' I credit a lot of that game to Gary.

"To be honest, that Auburn game had to be one of my biggest memories. Tackling Bo Jackson head to head had to be the biggest thrill for me. Afterward, when I saw the tackle on television, I thought, 'Man, here is a human phenom, and I'm out there tackling him one on one!'"

Call it a David and Goliath story if you like. I prefer to call it typical Michigan football.

I would pick out a jersey that was the wrong color

I n the mid-1960s, Frank Nunley used to roam the interior of the Wolverine defense. A native of Belleville, just down the road from Ann Arbor, Nunley was a middle linebacker by trade and a darn good one. He helped Michigan to a Rose Bowl appearance and victory in his sophomore year. He was named to the All-Big Ten first team in his senior year.

"I was very young when I got here," Nunley explains. "I was a year younger than most of the guys, so this is the way I used to play defense when I came here. I would pick out a jersey that was the wrong color, and I would go and knock it down. I would try and hurt it."

Home is where the heart is

L inebacker Frank Nunley went from his stellar career at Michigan Stadium to becoming a third-round draft choice of the San Francisco 49ers, a team he played on for 10 years. He now has settled in the Bay Area, but Ann Arbor always has a special place in his memory.

"You do not realize," Nunley says, "what a wonderful organization this is until you are older. When you are in high school, you don't look at things as closely as you do when you are older, like the tradition here.

"From the very first day that I walked on this campus, those coaches ragged on me all four years I was here to make sure I got my degree. They were great football coaches, too. A lot of them went on to very successful professional careers. We had great football teams, too, but they were on me about my degree. You realize after all of that, this is a way of life.

"Unfortunately, I ended up in the Bay Area, and I haven't been able to enjoy my Michigan experience as much as I probably should have over the past 10 or 15 years. When I come back to Ann Arbor, though, its like," Nunley pauses for a moment, "coming home. It feels like you're back home again."

Bo wants to see you

I have had the opportunity on a number of occasions to hear Bo Schembechler speak at numerous events. The organizers of these events usually ask Coach Schembechler to talk as a motivational speaker. He is an exceptional speaker at sales meetings or gatherings with business executives. He is engaging, funny, and opinionated. He uses his experience as a coach to teach lessons that can be used in business and in life. One of the stories he always uses at these speeches centers around the opening of his 1980 season at Michigan.

The Wolverines had lost two of their first three games and were clearly struggling. The captain on that team, Andy Cannavino, had complained openly that Coach was working them too hard and that the players weren't having any fun, so Coach Schembechler called Cannavino to his office and verbally took him apart. He had Cannavino in tears. Cannavino left his office and became the best captain he ever had. The team won nine straight and beat Washington in the Rose Bowl.

Coach Schembechler then tells his audience that the lesson learned in this story was about a failure of his. He says he failed to coach attitude, and he and his coaches never forgot that lesson from that moment on.

It is a great story, and according to Cannavino, it's pretty close to how he remembers it.

"Actually, about 90 percent of it is true," he admits. "To really understand the whole story, you've got to go back to the end of the previous season. We had lost our last three games of the previous year to Purdue, Ohio State, and North Carolina in the Gator Bowl. So we ended my junior year 0-3, and we started my senior year 1-2. Our only win was 17-10 over Northwestern, and I intercepted a pass in the end zone with about a minute to go, or they might have tied us."

It was a difficult time. Cannavino says he was frustrated. In class students were asking him what was wrong with the team.

One day during practice defensive coordinator Bill McCartney came up to him.

"Hey, what's going on with the team? What do you think is wrong?" he asked.

"You know, Mac, the guys are grumbling. We're working too hard," Cannavino said nonchalantly, explaining that the grueling hitting drills they were doing over and over again were hurting the morale of the young defense. "Practices are too long; nobody is having any fun."

Cannavino thought about second-year Ohio State coach Earl Bruce, who had opened the current season with three victories, and all of the fun the players were having under his leadership as opposed to what they had experienced under Woody Hayes. He looked at Coach McCartney, who he saw as a friend, and was completely honest about the temperament of the team.

At 7 a.m. the next day, Coach Schembechler's secretary called Cannavino.

"Bo wants to see you," she said.

Cannavino was surprised.

"I had no idea what he would want with me so early in the morning," Cannavino explains, "so I got dressed and went over at about 8 or 8:30. Bo's secretary met me, and then Bo opened his door and let me in his office. As soon as he closed the door, he started screaming at me!"

Cannavino sat down, facing the angry man across from him.

"How dare you tell us we're working too hard!" he screamed at Cannavino. "You're my captain! You've got to be me on the field! You want me to call up Reggie McKenzie and Dan Dierdorf and tell them I'm working *you* too hard!"

Cannavino was completely taken aback.

"I didn't think the comment I made to McCartney was that big a deal," he confesses years later. "I've got to tell you, I started crying. Tears were streaming down my face, and I didn't know what to say, because I literally didn't think I'd said anything that bad. But Bo was screaming. It went on for about 10 minutes. It seemed like an eternity to me."

Coach Schembechler finished his tirade in a way that stuck with Cannavino, "You're going to leave this room today, and you are going to be *me* on the field! You are going to become my greatest captain ever, and we are going to win every single game from here on in and that includes the Rose Bowl!"

Then he threw the captain out of his office.

"After I left that meeting," Cannavino confesses, "I actually did change. I became more vocal on the field. I gave more orders. To give you an example of how I changed, against Ohio State, Mike Trgovac, a defensive lineman, came into the game. He had been hurt during the week and had been in and out of practice, so when he came into the game, he asked me, 'What's the play? What's the play?' And I screamed at him, 'If you don't know the f------ play, then get out of here!'

"I think I really did become a good captain, and we ended up winning every game, and luckily for me, because we won Bo's first Rose Bowl and kind of got the monkey off his back, Bo tells the story about me becoming his greatest captain.

"It worked out really good for me, and to be honest, I think I got lucky."

Cannavino was the right guy at the right time. He endured a message from Coach Schembechler that not many could have survived. Not only did he survive, he improved. His performance after that meeting was a benchmark that Coach Schembechler and the staff felt needed to be recognized.

"At the end of the season," Cannavino says proudly, "just to show you that I think the coaches saw how much I changed, they gave me a plaque. It's a plaque that is dedicated to my leadership. A copy of it hangs in Schembechler Hall in Ann Arbor. I know they didn't give that to every captain, but they gave one to me. I really think they saw that I did become a better captain."

Besides the remarkable turnaround by Cannavino, Coach Schembechler himself changed his approach slightly. He needed to get practices re-energized. He had to find a way to make it fun again. Cannavino says Coach Schembechler went back to what he knew best.

"After that meeting that he had with me, he changed our practice schedule. We stretched at the beginning of practice, and right after that he blew the whistle and called the whole team together. He then lined up the first-team offensive front, and the first-team defensive front, and we would have a live scrimmage.

"I mean the offensive front was full of guys who would be drafted in the NFL in the first three rounds," Cannavino says, "and on defense, we were young, but we had Mel Owens, me, and Mike Trgovac. What that drill did was get us ready physically, but it also got us pumped up for practice. We had the offense on one side and the defense on the other, and we'd be screaming and yelling and going crazy for about 10 to 12 plays. That intensity and fun in that short drill made the rest of practice more fun. We did that every day for about five or six weeks. It became something we looked forward to."

It's all about attitude, friends. Don't ever forget to coach attitude.

I flipped him the bird

I ntensity and dedication are two traits that seem to be prerequisites for good linebackers, and there is no question that Andy Cannavino was a very good linebacker. His intensity at times got the better of him, though, especially against Ohio State.

Paul Girgash, another Michigan linebacker and friend of Cannavino's, called him a few years back. Girgash had phoned Cannavino because he had to get an explanation for something that Cannavino had supposedly done while in uniform during an Ohio State game.

"Girgash was at an Ohio State function," Cannavino explains, "and he met [former OSU coach] Earl Bruce. Well, Girgash and Bruce started reminiscing about the Michigan–Ohio State games."

Cannavino's name came up during the discussion.

"You know, that Cannavino was a hell of a linebacker, but he's kind of whacky, isn't he?" Bruce asked Girgash.

"What do you mean?" Girgash questioned in response.

"Cannavino gave me the finger during the Ohio State game when I was coaching!"

Right then Girgash knew he had to get to the bottom of this story.

"You've got to understand, my dad went to Ohio State and played under Woody Hayes," Cannavino explains, "and I only wanted to play for Woody Hayes and Ohio State, but they didn't recruit me or give me a scholarship. Bo did, so I went to Michigan. So all I ever wanted to do every year was beat Ohio State. In my senior year we were playing Ohio State in Columbus for the Big Ten title and the Rose Bowl. I was so emotional. I mean I was crying. I was so pumped up; it was unbelievable. I didn't even know where I was half the time. I was out of control.

"During the game at some point, there was a pass near the sidelines. I tipped the ball, and it rolled out of bounds on the Ohio State sidelines near Earl Bruce. When I got up, Bruce was about five feet away. I don't know what came over me, but I got up real quick, flipped him the bird, stared at him, and said something stupid.

"Believe me, I'm not proud of it. I was out of my mind in that game."

Intensity, huh? Yeah, I guess that explains it.

I scored and got ripped for it

Tom Seabron played from 1975 to 1978 and was a standout as an outside linebacker for the Wolverines in the years that Rick Leach and the offense were making headlines. To give you an example of how well the defense played in the four years Seabron and crew were roaming Michigan Stadium, get a load of these numbers; the most total points allowed for the season over that four-year span was 130. In 1976 over the course of 12 games, the defense gave up a total of 95 points and recorded five shutouts. In 1978 they gave up only 105 points in 12 games. They were a dominant group, and Seabron was a part of it right from his freshman year.

Seabron came to Michigan out of the Detroit Public School league. He was very athletic and was fast. Originally he had been slated to play tight end, but his athleticism and speed got the coaches thinking, and they moved him to outside linebacker/defensive end not long into his freshman campaign. It was during that freshman campaign that Seabron's moment in the sun would arrive. The dream of every youngster who plays the game came Seabron's way, and he made the best of it.

"Actually, it was the first game I got a chance to play in," he says, "and it was against Northwestern. The score when I got into the game was 62-0 in our favor. The Northwestern quarterback at that particular time was running an option offense. It was kind of the norm in those days. A lot of teams ran option football.

"Anyway, as the quarterback came toward me on the option, I was doing the cat and mouse with him, and I leaped at the same moment he pitched the ball. His hand and my hand met the ball together. Rather than just tackling him, I grabbed the ball, spun off, and ran 40 or 50 yards for a touchdown.

"As I was running in for the touchdown, I got to about the 20-yard line and held the ball over my head as I ran the last 20 yards for the score."

It was a dream come true, getting a fumble like that and scoring in his first game. It clearly was looking like the first highlight in a long list of them in Seabron's career. It was a ticket to becoming a regular sub and then maybe a starter. His football future looked bright. Then came a crash of reality.

Head coach Bo Schembechler wasn't cheering.

"He went crazy on me the next day at our Sunday meeting," Seabron says while laughing.

"He yelled, 'How could you do that?!!? We don't do that at Michigan!'"

Coach Schembechler always preached winning with class, and holding the ball over his head the last 20 yards was Seabron's mistake. The head coach saw that as rubbing it in, and that was unacceptable.

"Obviously he was embarrassed because my touchdown had made the final score 69-0 over Northwestern," Seabron explains. "So he just ripped me to shreds. I thought I had done something well, but I learned something else instead. He was setting the tone for a freshman what this four-year experience was going to be like. There wasn't going to be any such thing as adulation or gloating, because in Bo's mind, he was the perfectionist. He was going to always drive you to be the perfect player. The best player you could be."

Seabron learned that lesson well. He became as good as he could be. He got drafted into the NFL by the San Francisco 49ers after his senior year. He had a nice career as a pro and is now back in his hometown as a very successful executive with Smith Barney.

And to think it all started with a fumble return for a touchdown at Michigan Stadium. Seabron, though, has a wonderful take on the whole incident.

"It was pretty much all downhill from there in terms of scoring," Seabron laughs, "because I never scored again. Can you believe it? That was the only touchdown I scored in my entire career, and I got ripped for it!"

We're going to get one thing straight

In the mid-1970s, recruiting was still the lifeblood of the football program. Duffy Daugherty had been the coach at Michigan State, and he was a charismatic and very popular in the state of Michigan. Coach Daugherty, who stopped coaching in 1972, had been winning the recruiting battle in the state, attracting a lot of Michigan's top talent away from Ann Arbor and coach Bo Schembechler. The former Spartan still cast a large shadow over the state's high school football talent base. Although Coach Schembechler had always been very good at convincing talented players to become Wolverines, his recruiting base at the time was more in Ohio than Michigan, because he came to the Michigan job from Miami of Ohio.

In 1975, an opportunity presented itself to take back the recruiting trail for Michigan, and Coach Schembechler was ready to take it. Tom Seabron was one of the major talents who watched it happen before his eyes.

Seabron just happened to make his official visit to Ann Arbor on a pretty big weekend for recruits when he was a senior in high school.

"The five guys who were there the same weekend," Seabron recalls, "were Rick Leach, Gene Johnson, Curt Greer, Harlan Huckleby, and me. Huck and Curt and I were all from Cass Tech in Detroit, and Rick and Gene were from Flint."

Coach Schembechler had to be salivating over the prospects of getting these five athletes into Maize and Blue jerseys. All of them were first-class students and football players; it was a homegrown gold mine for Schembechler, and it was his chance to pull the coup de grace on MSU that could put him on the map in the very fertile recruiting grounds of Michigan.

On Sunday morning Coach Schembechler invited all five prospects into his office for a heart-to-heart chat before they left for home. As he closed the door after the youngsters entered, he looked at them.

"We're going to get one thing straight, right now!" he said straightforwardly. "I want a commitment from you five guys today. You five guys are going to be the key to Michigan football. All of you are in-state All-State players, and I want commitments."

He turned to Leach.

"Where are you going to school, Rick?"

"Michigan."

And he continued down the line.

"Where are you going to school, Curt?"

"Michigan."

"Where are you going to school, Gene?"

"Michigan."

"Where are you going to school, Harlan?"

"Michigan."

He turned to Seabron and asked the same question.

"Where are you going to school, Tom?"

"I don't know."

Coach Schembechler stared at him and did not look too happy.

"How can you, at this moment, with all these other guys committing to Michigan still tell me you don't know?" he stated rather loudly.

"I just am not ready to commit," the young recruit responded.

The boys left the office, and Michigan continued to go after Seabron, but Seabron continued to hold out.

"The turning point came when I had a private meeting with Bo at his home," Seabron explains. "At the time, I had narrowed my choices down between Michigan and Tennessee. And to be honest, I was still talking to guys like Conredge Holloway and Bill Battle of Tennessee. Bo knew I was still interested in Tennessee when I met him at his home. So he gave me a history lesson about the black athlete.

"He proceeded to tell me how Michigan had recruited black athletes in the 1920s and the 1930s, 1940s, and 1950s. He told me I was a Northern guy and I should begin to understand Tennessee. He said, 'I don't think Tennessee got their first African-American athlete until somewhere in the mid-1960s,'" Seabron remembers. "He explained all about the SEC to me. Then he gave me the history of Michigan. He brought up Julius Franks, a black All-American at Michigan in the early 1940s. He mentioned Lowell Perry and Jimmy Pace, who were 1950s All-Americans for Michigan. He went on to tell me that the Big Ten was the first conference to admit the black athlete, and how could I be from Detroit and tell him I wanted to go to Tennessee?

"When I came back from that visit with Bo, it kind of put Tennessee in perspective in terms of what was important to me. Not that back then race or culture was such a big deal like it is sometimes today. But Bo taught me something about the South that I hadn't thought about before.

"I have joked with Bo years later that he played the race card on Tennessee. He laughs when I tell him that, but he really understood recruiting, and he had some phenomenal assistant coaches. But it was Bo who had a way about him that truly made you begin to understand what he was building and what Michigan was representing."

By landing Seabron and the class that included Leach, Johnson, Greer, and Huckleby, Coach Schembechler never had a hint of a problem recruiting in the state of Michigan ever again.

"The next year, we got Roosevelt Smith, Mike Harden, and Ron Simpkins all out of Detroit," Seabron explains. "We cleaned up in Detroit. We got whomever we wanted out of Detroit."

And Michigan kept winning football games. The two went hand in hand.

CHAPTER TWELVE

Defensive Backs

I came through

When Miami of Ohio threatened to come back late in the game during the 2004 opener, Ernest Shazor was there.

He stepped in front of a Redhawk pass, nabbed it, and returned it 88 yards for a touchdown that broke Miami's back and secured a win for Michigan.

When Purdue challenged Michigan's two-point lead and run for the Big Ten championship, Shazor was there, too.

With just over two minutes to play, he swooped down on a Purdue receiver who was barreling toward the Michigan goal line and stripped the ball away. The Wolverines recovered the fumble, ending Purdue's chances and securing victory for the Maize and Blue.

But ironically those game-making plays that experts attribute as his memorable moments are not what stand out to him as the ultimate career highlight.

"It was the Minnesota game [in 2004 season]," Shazor explains. "I had 12 tackles in that game. But late in the game when we needed the ball back, I made three tackles in a row for a loss. That had to be one of my biggest moments in Michigan Stadium. There wasn't much time left, and Minnesota was driving. I had to come up with some big plays, and I came through for the team."

The operative words there are *came through for the team*. It was all about the team. That's why it's unforgettable. When the team wins, Shazor wins.

There was some bitterness

W hen your good friends make great plays in games, I can guarantee that you remember everything about it. In our sophomore year against Illinois, Bruce Elliott, a classmate of mine and a good friend, made one of those great plays, but it wasn't until 35 years later that I found out the inside detail that makes the moment even more remarkable.

In 1969 the Fighting Illini were led by head coach Jim Valek, who had replaced Pete Elliott, Bruce's father, as the Illinois coach a year earlier. The unpleasantness of Pete Elliott's firing occurred as Elliott was being recruited and making his choice to attend Michigan. So as a fellow freshman recruit, I lived through the firing with him to some degree. Most of the recruits from our class had met Coach Elliott, and to a man we all had great respect for him. He was a class act, and as 18-year-old kids, none of us felt very positive about Illinois, considering what they had done to our friend's dad.

It wasn't just us, either. Elliott says the mood in Champaign was not unanimous about his dad's termination either.

"To say the least," Elliott remembers, "there was some bitterness involved. It wasn't necessarily all the people at Illinois, but a few people at Illinois. The fans and most of the athletic department were supportive of my father, but a few were not supportive, and unfortunately, he was asked to leave."

Going into the game against Illinois our sophomore year, the feelings surrounding Coach Elliott's firing were still raw for us. Every single player on the Michigan squad wanted Elliott to get into that game and play well to exact his revenge.

We were leading something like 50-0, and the call for the reserves went out. Suddenly Elliott the benchwarmer was now playing cornerback in a Michigan victory at Illinois. But that was not enough to satisfy Elliott's desire for payback.

Late in the game, Illinois was trying to avoid a shutout when they threw a pass in Elliott's direction. Elliott went up for the ball and grabbed it.

Then he zigged to the opposite side of the field dodging tacklers; then he zagged the other way. He was in a free-for-all run and headed straight for the end zone.

Once he got there, the entire Michigan bench emptied onto the field to mob Elliott in celebration. (If the excessive celebration penalty were in force back then, we'd have been flagged twice!)

"I do remember a lot of people coming out there," Elliott chuckles. "As a matter of fact, it was so tumultuous that somebody's slapping me on the back actually knocked my contact lens out of my eye!

"I really appreciated all the support from the team. It was one of the great moments in my life. But, you know another amazing thing, my dad told me that as soon as I intercepted the ball, the Illinois fans in the stands realized what was happening and they got up and started to cheer, even though their team was getting beaten by 50! A little unusual, but nice.

"You may not believe this," Elliott imparts the heretofore unknown fact with a grin, "but I actually had a dream about it the night before the game. I'm serious. In our hotel in Champaign, I had a dream that I was going to intercept a pass and return it for a touchdown. I really wanted to do something extraordinary in the game, and as it worked out, it couldn't have been better."

They used broomsticks

During the late 1980s Michigan had two safeties—Tripp Welborne and Vada Murray—who had the uncanny ability to block kicks. If you were watching Michigan football games in those years at Michigan Stadium, you had to have noticed them. They appeared as if they were shot out of a cannon, flew over the line of scrimmage with their arms outstretched, and got a piece of a field goal attempt. Whether it was their timing or their leaping ability, they were good at it. And they both knew it.

"It got to the point where Tripp and I started to compete against each other to see who could jump the highest," Murray kids. "Tripp always said that the photographers never snapped the pictures of them leaping over the pile at his highest point. He always thought he had an extra burst. The truth was, I could just out-jump him."

But before the competition developed, the two had to convince defensive coordinator Lloyd Carr to let them try to be on the field goal defense unit.

"We talked to him about letting us try it," Murray explains. "Lloyd wasn't too sure at first, so he went to Bo and talked about it. That week in practice, we tried it over and over, and after they saw what we could do, they said, 'Okay, let's give it a shot.' And we started blocking kicks."

Murray and Welborne got so good at blocking kicks that Michigan's opponents actually started to plan against them.

"I think the one team that really came up with a good effort to try and stop us," Murray recalls with a smile, "was Southern California in the Rose Bowl. We were told that when they practiced extra points and field goals, they had tall guys standing behind the line of scrimmage with broomsticks held up in the air trying to block the kicks! Their coach apparently said they didn't have anybody who could jump as high as Tripp or I could."

Tripp Welborne, No. 3, and Vada Murray, No. 27, were so good at blocking kicks that teams resorted to players holding broomsticks to simulate Welborne's and Murray's jumping ability.

Commiting to Bump

George Hoey came to Michigan in the mid-1960s from Flint, Michigan. He had been heavily recruited by Michigan State, Ohio State, Missouri, and Purduc, but it was Michigan and head coach Bump Elliott who made the best impression.

Coach Elliott came to the Hoey home and did not promise the valued recruit the world. He was upfront and honest about what Michigan had to offer the young running back.

"George, I'm going to level with you," Coach Elliott stated straightforwardly. "We want you to come to Michigan on a full scholarship. You will come to school as a running back, but we have Jim Detwiler and Carl Ward in front of you. You aren't going to play for probably two years. But we still want you at Michigan. You will get a great education."

Hoey immediately committed to Michigan and canceled the visits he had planned to other schools. He knew the Maize and Blue were for him.

"Bump had made a commitment to me," Hoey explain. "It was his pure honesty, his legitimacy that I bought into. That, to me, is what represents Michigan. It always has and always will. And I loved every moment of my time here."

Shortly after staking his claim with the Wolverines, Missouri head coach Dan Devine called Hoey to double-check that Hoey was planning to visit Columbia to check out Mizzou.

"Are you coming to visit?" he began.

"No," Hoey replied. "I have committed to Michigan."

Coach Devine was quiet for a moment before he said, "Can't fault that decision."

If he were smart,
he wouldn't have fielded that ball

Sometimes the exploits of the modern-day player obscure some pretty fair accomplishments from those of the past. We have been blessed at Michigan with some unbelievable kick return experts. The names of Woodson, Howard, Carter, and Breaston have almost erased the memories of some exceptional return specialists. One of the names not to be forgotten while looking back into Michigan football history is George Hoey.

It wasn't long after he came to Michigan that the young running back was moved to defensive back, and it wasn't long after that he was setting records as a punt return threat. Hoey is still featured in the Michigan record books for most return yardage in a game. He holds the third and fifth spots in the top five list, and the other two Michigan players who appear with him on that list are Tom Harmon and Anthony Carter. So Hoey is in select company, and his status as a return specialist is as solid as concrete in the Michigan record books.

Hoey was so good in his junior and senior years that he became a marked man. Sometimes his frustration at being a marked man forced him into some extraordinary decisions.

"I know it was in the Navy game, either my junior or senior year," Hoey recalls. "It was a time when teams would not kick it to me. They would kick it away from me out of bounds. Finally the Navy punter punted one to me. By all rights, I should have fair-caught the ball. It was only about a 30- or 40-yard punt. Well, I took it back for about 69 yards and a score. But I remember the Navy coach saying afterward, 'If he were a smart football player, he wouldn't have fielded that ball.' Maybe I wasn't that smart."

You didn't want to get undressed

For Jeff Cohen the entire 1980 season was the most memorable time of his life. It was a year in which Michigan opened with a win and then lost the next two. They were 1-2 after three games, and at that point, a lot of folks, including the media, had written Michigan off. But what nobody ever took into account was the resolve of a group of athletes and the faith of a coaching staff. Cohen was on that team, and he says the journey was full of moments that ultimately trumped the end result.

"I'll never forget," Cohen starts, "after we were 1-2, Bo had a meeting and told us we were going to shut off the outside world. We were not going to talk to the media. We were not going to care what people said. We were going to take with us the 'us against the world' mentality the rest of the year.

"When we went down to Indiana to play, we were 5-2, but Indiana had one of their best teams in a long time, and before the game, it was the first time I can ever remember Bo gathering up the team and telling us we had to take the approach that today we were going to go out and take over the stadium. Basically, he said this was going to be *our* stadium. We went out and beat Indiana 35-0. For the rest of the season, our mindset was simple. We took over whatever stadium we were playing, and we would dominate.

"And Bo kept reminding us, 'I told you guys when we were 1-2 that I still thought we were good enough to win the championship, and that if you will believe in us as coaches and yourselves as a team, it will happen!' It was like a snowball; it just steamrolled. Our defense was unbelievable, and our offense was clicking."

The team kept on clicking, and after they beat Ohio State in Columbus 9-3 to secure the Big Ten championship, the bedlam and joy in the locker room was striking. For 30 minutes, not a single person took off a pad or a jersey—the players kept screaming, hugging, and celebrating as everyone got a rose. They were all caught up in the moment.

"That, to me, is probably the greatest moment that I recall in a postgame locker room," Cohen exclaims. "You just didn't want to get undressed! You wanted to savor that moment.

"It was such a great moment that even though we went out to Pasadena and won the Rose Bowl, it almost felt anticlimactic. Don't get me wrong; it was great, but I didn't have the same feeling winning the Rose Bowl as I did in going down to Columbus and winning that game and the Big Ten title."

CHAPTER THIRTEEN

Overtime

Crisler and Lindbergh

One of the morning anchors for WWJ All News Radio is Joe Donovan. Donovan is an absolute football junkie; he knows every team's nickname and their fight song, no matter how obscure the school. He used to anchor a football scoreboard show Saturday afternoons that ran before and after the broadcast of the Michigan games. Donovan loved doing that show. He put as much of his heart and soul into those scoreboard shows as he did with anything else he'd ever done.

Donovan is also a huge Michigan fan. So it was after my first book came out and Donovan had read it when we met in the parking lot at WWJ Radio one day.

"Hey Jim, read the book and loved it," Donovan told me.
"Thanks, Joe," I responded, "coming from a football maniac like you, that is high praise indeed."
"You know," Donovan continued. "You should have included the story about Fritz Crisler being picked up as a possible suspect in the Lindbergh kidnapping."
My jaw just about hit the pavement of the parking lot.
"What?" I said incredulously.
"Yeah," Donovan said with a knowing chuckle. "I read it in a book about Ivy League football. I'll get it for you."
Sure enough, a few days later Donovan dropped off the book, *Football: The Ivy League, Origins of an American Obsession.* The book was written by Mark F. Bernstein in 2001. It discusses the origins of American football and how instrumental the Ivy League was in creating what is known today as college football.
Most of us know that before Fritz Crisler became legendary at Michigan, he had an exceptional career before he arrived in Ann Arbor. An All-America end at the University of Chicago in 1921, Crisler also was a solid basketball and baseball player at the school, even getting a brief tryout with the Chicago White Sox of Major League Baseball after he graduated.
Football, though, was Crisler's first love. He served as an assistant coach to the venerable Amos Alonzo Stagg for eight years. Then he went on to the University of Minnesota as the Gophers' head coach for two years. It was after his second year in Minneapolis that Crisler was sought out by Princeton of the Ivy League to be their new head football coach.
Clearly, football in the East, and, in particular, the Ivy League was the pinnacle of the game at that time in history. Princeton, according to Bernstein's book, was desperate to get their program back up and competitive after a dismal one-win season in 1931. The university had even considered hiring Knute Rockne before he was tragically killed in a plane crash. So Princeton took a chance on Crisler to lead their football program in 1932.
Crisler came to Princeton to finalize his contract on March 1, 1932. At dawn the next morning he borrowed a car to get

Fritz Crisler hardly looks like a suspicious person, does he?

back to the train station from where he was scheduled to return to Minneapolis. He was unfamiliar with the roads and got lost when the police found him and took him into custody.

The police were combing the area because hours before Charles Lindbergh's infant son had been abducted in a town called Hopewell, which was about 10 miles away. They questioned Crisler about his whereabouts, and it wasn't until the man Crisler had borrowed the car from came and vouched for him that he was released.

Fortunately his tenure at Princeton was not as ominous as its beginnings. Although the Michigan star was the first non-alumnus to ever coach at the school and there were some grumblings amongst the Princeton faithful, the complaints were short lived. In six seasons at Princeton, Crisler produced 35 wins against only nine losses and five ties.

Football was secondary

S ometimes Michigan football isn't about the sport; it's about the sports coat.

Vada Murray and the team went to Pasadena for the Rose Bowl, and while they were there, they attended a party, the Big Ten Dinner of Champions, hosted by Bob Hope at the Hollywood Palladium. At the dinner table, many of the players took off their sports coats and hung them on the backs of their chairs. The players did not think anything of it.

"Well, the next day at practice," Murray recalls, "that's all Bo [Schembechler] could talk about. He told us how inappropriate that was, and how in the business world when you get out of college you don't do that.

"Right then and there, that told me, as far as being at Michigan, football was secondary. Bo was getting us ready for life."

Restitution completed

I n January 2003, I received a letter from a John Mooney of Bad Axe, Michigan. Mr. Mooney is a history teacher at Harbor Beach High School and a very avid Michigan football fan. In his letter, Mr. Mooney wrote that he had attended his first game at The Big House in October 1963 and has been hooked ever since.

Mr. Mooney's daughter, Erin, who at the time was an engineering student at Michigan and completing her third year in the marching band, had given her father the first *Tales from Michigan Stadium* to read. Mr. Mooney was very complimentary in his review, and I was very pleased. As I read on though, I got a surprise. One of the stories had a factual error in it, and Mr. Mooney wanted to make me aware of it. What follows is a portion of that letter explaining the mistake.

I enjoyed every minute of your book! Nevertheless, what I was intrigued with most was Bob Chappuis's recollection concerning "The Pride of Harbor Springs."

Is it true that memory improves with age? Actually, there is about a 100-mile mistake differential (as the crow flies) in the tackle-dodging yarn spinner's remembrance. While Coach Crisler might have said, "[Jim] Brieske, you're not the pride of Harbor Springs, you're a jack-ass."—I would like to go on record in saying that we in Harbor Beach take exception! Jim Brieske is our "jack-ass"—not Harbor Springs'—and we'd like him back!! I trust you are taking this in the spirit it is intended!!

Not only is Harbor Beach noted for being the home of Frank Murphy and James Lincoln (both with U of M roots, and being the only two men to have court buildings in Michigan named after them,) Jim Brieske is also an alumnus—a June 1941 graduate of Harbor Beach High School.

Now, as far as the matter of restitution—in order to put the Beach back on the map concerning Wolverine lore, perhaps a mention in "Tales 2" would be fitting.

Go Blue,
John M. Mooney

First of all Mr. Mooney, the mistake is all mine, not Mr. Chappuis's.

Regarding restitution, consider that mention a done deal.

We were not called cheerleaders

I n September 1974 the headlines in the *Ann Arbor News* and the *Detroit News* read, "A U-M Tradition crumbles!"

What sacred tradition had been ended?

The Wolverine mascot? The singing of "The Victors"? The colors Maize and Blue?

According to the articles, the time of the all-male cheerleading squad had come to an end. Women were going to be allowed on the sidelines to show their spirit and pump up the crowd.

But what seems like a natural evolution turned into a mini-sexual revolution as the women on the squad had to face the angst surrounding the change.

"There was some resentment," admits Clare Canham-Eaton, the daughter of Michigan athletic director Don Canham and a member of the initial unit. "It was definitely controversial, because we were breaking such a long-standing tradition. The male cheerleaders weren't too thrilled with us, but it was the alumni who were not happy at all!

"I remember there were letters to the editor and editorials in the newspaper about us. And in that first game, one of the girls got hit with a can of pop thrown from the stands. The student section actually booed us! At the beginning, it was not a pleasant situation. We had two security guards with us all the time."

At one point, Canham-Eaton's father, Don Canham, had to call a meeting.

"Both the male and female squads met with Canham," remembers Pat Perry, the squad's adviser and wife of sports information director Will Perry, "and Don said, so everybody clearly understood, 'This is going to come to pass, and we are going to have both squads on the field!'"

Perry was adamant that her squad belonged on the field at Michigan Stadium. She told the *Ann Arbor News* at the time,

"How many years ago was it that girls were finally allowed to walk through the front door of the Student Union? When I was a student, I had to walk through the side door."

But the men on the squad were not pleased, and they made that known by issuing some ground rules for their compliance to share the sideline with the women.

"First of all," Canham-Eaton says with a can-you-believe-it? smile. "We were told that we were not cheerleaders! That was a huge, huge point. We were told we had to call ourselves pom-pom girls!"

And it didn't stop there. The girls were to stay on the south side of the field and were not allowed to come down to where the boys were cheering. They were forbidden from starting a cheer; they could only join in after the all-male squad had begun one. They also could not let go of the gold and blue pom-poms they were required to hold—to emphasize that they were only a "pom-pom" squad. Clutching those pom-poms for four straight hours caused their skin to turn blue.

The road was no less friendly a place for the female troupe.

"We only went to one road game that first year," Canham-Eaton says, "and that was Ohio State. Well, the morning of the game we got dressed in our uniforms at a nearby hotel, and we all got in the van to drive to the game. We had a press parking credential, but we didn't know where the parking lot was located. So as we got close to the stadium, we stopped and asked an Ohio state trooper where we had to go to find this particular lot. When he looked at us in our Michigan uniforms inside the van, he paused, and said, 'The only place you can go to—is hell.' Isn't that wild? Then, before the game was over, our two security guards whisked us out of the stadium, Yeah, we were moved out long before the final gun. And on our way out of Columbus as we were driving home, we stopped at a restaurant to eat. We hadn't eaten all day. We were still in our uniforms, and the waitress at this restaurant refused to serve us!"

Perry had no budget for the girl's squad and had to beg, borrow, and steal to get them into appropriate attire. She once borrowed waitress uniforms from Weber's Hotel for a performance. And she put an ad in the *Ann Arbor News* to secure some long-legged white go-go boots that the girls needed for a number they were scheduled to perform with the band. The ad worked, and the performance went on as scheduled.

It was also determined that the pom-pom squad would be affiliated with the band to distance them even more from cheerleader status. That separation actually helped the whole plan work. Band director George Cavender was very supportive of the women's squad. Cavender saw it as another entertainment opportunity. He even prepared and rehearsed special numbers for the female unit.

Eventually it all blew over.

"By the end of the year," Canham-Eaton recalls, "there was no controversy.

"I absolutely loved it. It was very fun. It's an incredible, incredible experience. I was awe-inspired by where I was and what I was a part of. I loved it because it gave me the opportunity to be a part of the great Michigan tradition. And now we realize that we were breaking tradition and making tradition at the same time. It was just great."

CHAPTER FOURTEEN

Legends

I scored on the Old 83 play

In 1954 the Wolverines were one win away from the Rose Bowl when they faced coach Woody Hayes and Hopalong Cassidy in Columbus. Michigan scored first, putting the Maize and Blue up 7-0.

"You see, I scored our first and only touchdown that counted in that game on the Old 83 play," halfback Danny Cline explains with a smile. "It was a fancy play where we faked the end around. Kramer went one way, and I went one way, then the other, and [Lou] Baldacci hit me with a high pass and I scored from about 10 yards out."

On the next possession the Wolverine offense stormed down the field again and made it to the Buckeye goal line. Captain Ted Cachey says the sequence started with an injury. "Coach Oosterbaan thought that our fullback, Fred Baer, was hurt, so Baer was on the bench, and Dave Hill was in Fred's spot at fullback. We got down to their three-yard line, and [we] had three cracks at the goal line and didn't score."

Or did they?

"Hey," Cline states emphatically, "I think Davey Hill got over the goal line on both of his carries! I was over, too. If you looked at it from the side, there was no doubt about it. *I was in the end zone,* and the ref said my knee touched down on the six-inch line."

That no call allowed Ohio State to stay in the game and ultimately win 21-7.

"If our score would have been allowed," Cline concludes, "we'd have gone up 14-0. Ohio State would not have come back from that, I'm sure of it."

Fifty years later the players still feel the injustice of that moment—but enough time has passed that they can laugh about it now when they get together at reunions.

"You know the line judge in that game who missed the call was at my wedding!" end Dave Rentschler confesses. "I told him on my wedding day that if he would have made the right call, I would have played in the Rose Bowl."

Cachey then chimes in so all can hear his retort.

"You know guys," Cachey says, "there may have been a reason that they didn't allow the score. If we'd have gone to the Rose Bowl, we would have all met movie stars, and we would not have married our wives. Our whole lives would have been changed!"

Everybody laughed at that one, especially the wives.

Put Bowman in!

The final home game for seniors is emotional for anyone who has ever worn the Maize and Blue. In 1954 Dan Cline and his classmates faced off against Michigan State for their final bout at Michigan Stadium. It was a great show as 97,239 faithful showed up to cheer them on. It was the largest crowd of the season, and they got to watch their beloved Michigan tear apart the Spartans in a rout.

But there was one moment in the game that stood out beyond the final score of 33-7 and the touchdown passes.

"I threw a pass to Lou Baldacci, and he went 67 yards for a touchdown," Cline recalls with pride, "and that kind of broke Michigan State's back. It was fairly late in the game, so they pulled me out, and I was sitting on the bench with tears running down my face."

On the bench next to him was his roommate and third-string center, Jim Bowman, who had never played in a game. Cline sat next to his friend and continued to sob because it was his last game as head coach Bennie Oosterbaan approached them.

"What is the matter?" he asked.

"Put Bowman in," Cline pleaded.

The head coach looked at Cline and turned to the bench-warmer next to him.

"Get in there, Bowman!" he shouted, pointing toward the field.

No. 52 trotted out onto the field, played the rest of the game, and earned his letter.

"He was so happy," Cline remembers. "And it goes to show you the kind of guy Bennie was. He was a guy you wanted to play for. He was never nasty to you to get you to play. He was the kind of coach you wanted to bust your tail for, not the kind of coach that would bust your tail for you. Bennie was just wonderful."

I held the money

Dave Rentschler was barely a teenager when one of his first memories about his many days at Michigan Stadium was seared into his consciousness.

"It was the 1946 Army game," Rentschler says proudly, "and I was ushering in section 23, where Boy Scout Troop 244 got to usher every week. So I was sitting there, and two men grabbed me. They told me to sit between them.

"So as I sat down between these two guys, they gave me what I remember to be $100. That was a lot of money! I hadn't held that much money very often. They told me to hold it. They said they'd tell me what to do with it near the end of the game.

"And near the end of the game, one guy turned to me and said, 'Okay give me the money.'

"The other guy looked at me and said, 'Go ahead, give it to him.'

"So I gave it to him, and it was all over with."

Rentschler got an early lesson in the art of the point spread, but it was also the first real lasting memory he has of the great Stadium, and it came a full five or six years before he ever played there. Not only did Rentschler get his first taste of the idea of gambling, he also got a taste of great college football.

"That was the game when I got to see Glenn Davis and 'Doc' Blanchard," Rentschler says matter-of-factly, as if the game happened yesterday. "Davis went on a 57-yard run for a touchdown, and Blanchard scored on a short run in an Army 20-13 victory."

The memory is clear as crystal. That should tell you something about the impact that game had on a young 13-year-old Boy Scout.

Two for a nickel or three for a dime

Howard Wikel is a lifelong Ann Arbor resident and the son of an Ann Arbor pharmacist and drugstore owner, whose life literally spans more than 70 years of history at the Michigan athletic department. The Michigan graduate and letter winner is an athletic department insider and has been since he was 10 years old.

Wikel's drugstore was located on the corner of East University and South University, across from the engineering

arch. As a youngster of about 12 or 13 years old, Wikel used to
spend time with his dad in the store when he became friendly
with one of the legends of college football, and the father of the
Michigan program, Fielding H. Yost.

Wikel got to know what Yost was like. He sat with Yost and
watched him interact with students.

"Mr. Yost knew my father very well, and he lived near the
store," Wikel remembers, "and he would come in quite often. As
you entered our store, immediately to the left was a cigar counter, and a little farther into the store there was a table with chairs
around it and a bench. Well, Mr. Yost would come in and he
would buy the most inexpensive cigars he could, two for a nick-
el or three for a dime, then he would go over and sit on the
bench at the table."

Yost at the time had retired from his coaching duties at
Michigan. His last year as the head coach was 1926, but he was
still managing the athletic department. As a matter of fact, he
never coached a game at Michigan Stadium. When the Stadium
opened, he was the athletic director; Tad Wieman was the first
Michigan coach at Michigan Stadium.

Clearly though, according to Wikel, Yost could not get
coaching out of his system.

"While Mr. Yost was sitting at this table chewing on his
cigar," Wikel recalls, "students would come in and go to the
front counter or the soda fountain. Occasionally, Mr. Yost
would call to one of them, 'Say, Laddie, why don't you sit down
for a moment? I'd like to talk to you.'"

What Yost did next was pure theater, according to Wikel.

"When the student sat down, he would take the salt and
pepper shakers, and any silverware or glasses on the table and
arrange them in a battleground setup from a famous Civil War
battle. He would then explain to the student, how you would
win the battle, using the assorted utensils on the table as troops.
He was a great expert on the Civil War.

"When he was done, Yost would then compare the strategy
used in winning the battle to the strategy used in running a
football play. He would explain how you needed to protect your
flanks and how you determined the weaknesses of your oppo-

A young Fielding Yost certainly embodies a legend to be.

nent and so on. When he got through with this lesson, Yost would ask the student if he understood these concepts. If the student said, 'Yes,' Yost then asked if he played checkers."

Apparently, more than a few students joined Yost for a game of checkers after the lesson, and as the checkers game went on,

Yost imparted more football wisdom to his young protégé. It made for some lively times in Mr. Wikel's drugstore.

"One of the problems that existed with Mr. Yost," Wikel confesses, "was that he could not accept the fact that he was no longer the coach. On occasion, when he would go to watch practice, he would literally walk on the field and start coaching part of the team! He wasn't the coach anymore, but he would go out there and start coaching.

"No one wanted to say no to him, but finally, someone did get to him, and said, 'Thank you, sir, but no thanks.'"

When the message finally hit home, Yost probably grumbled about it. He only wanted what was best for Michigan, and he still thought he was the best. A guy who accomplished as much as he did had to have enormous self-confidence.

To this day, we still feel and see the impact of Yost's genius all over the Michigan campus. That's why Howard Wikel is so valuable to us. He is the window through which we get to meet the great man.

As soft a sell as there ever was

Dave Rentschler was a young man torn. On the one side, he had the Technicolor memories of Michigan games and practices, and players and glory from when his dad, a referee, would take him to the Stadium or practice field.

Imagine the thrill as a young teenager getting to go to a Michigan practice. When coach Fritz Crisler would bring in a referee to work a practice scrimmage occasionally, that referee was Dave Rentschler's father. Rentschler never missed the chance to go along with his dad, and there were moments at practices that remain etched in his memory.

"One of my biggest thrills at practice," Rentschler grins, "was pulling Roger Zatkoff's jersey over his head. He was late to practice and couldn't get his jersey up over his pads by himself. Here I was a kid standing on the side, and I was able to help him get his jersey on."

And having a father as a referee also helped Rentschler see some of the most talented collegiate players the country had to offer.

"I got to see Norm Van Brocklin play quarterback for Oregon. He came into Michigan Stadium and played.

"I saw Michigan State come in with Muddy Waters as their 23-year-old freshman quarterback. They wore black and gold with a red 'S' on their helmets in the middle of their forehead instead of on the side. Two years later, my dad refereed the Michigan–Michigan State game when they came in with a team dressed in splendid white uniforms with green trim. Lynn Chandnois and those guys played for them at the time. I remember Michigan won that game."

With such a deep connection to the glory days, it was thought that Rentschler would have been sold on becoming a Wolverine. But he had even older memories of his childhood in Cleveland, and some family members who cheered for the Buckeyes of Ohio State filled him with stories about Woody Hayes and the Horseshoe.

"I came from a family with some mixed blood," Rentschler confesses.

He was leaning toward Ohio State when head coach Bennie Oosterbaan got a hold of him. A fine athlete, Coach Oosterbaan knew Rentschler would be an asset to Michigan, and he wanted his talents in Maize and Blue.

Coach Oosterbaan, of course, was already an icon in Ann Arbor. In the mid-1920s, he was considered one of the greatest college players ever. As a coach, he was very player friendly. He was an assistant coach for 20 years at Michigan. He learned his craft under two masters, Harry Kipke and Fritz Crisler. So Coach Oosterbaan was as well prepared as anyone when he was selected to be Michigan's head coach in 1948. Replacing Coach Crisler was not going to be the easiest of jobs, but Coach Oosterbaan was more than up to it. As a matter of fact, Coach Oosterbaan followed Coach Crisler's national title in 1947 with a national championship of his own in 1948.

Continuing this dynasty, though, meant bringing in great players every year. Coach Oosterbaan was very different from

Coach Crisler in his approach. While Coach Crisler was gruff and very demanding, Coach Oosterbaan was very kind, almost to a fault. As Michigan's legendary Ron Kramer, who played for Oosterbaan, once said, "Bennie was such a gentle soul." But it was that gentle approach of Coach Oosterbaan's that Rentschler said was appealing.

"Bennie was as soft a sell as there ever was," Rentschler says with great respect. "He just liked to talk to you about Michigan. He would come up to you, put his hand on your shoulder, ask how you were doing, ask how football was coming, and say things like, 'We sure hope you enjoy yourself here.' He talked to my dad a few times, too. When I finally decided to go to Michigan, it felt so good. It was as if I was destined to go there. Bennie made it feel like home to me. He made me feel like I belonged."

Freshmen were separate

It is not easy being a freshman, and apparently in the mid-1950s, it was even harder.

"You were a *freshman*," Dave Rentschler explains emphatically. "Freshmen were separate from the varsity, and as a freshman, you had to handle it that way. I remember there was a big cart with a pile of crushed leather helmets. They were all old painted up leather headgear. We would crowd around the cart and try and pick a helmet that fit each night for practice. When practice was over, we would throw the helmets back in the cart. The next day, we'd try to find the same one or get one close to it and practice again."

One of the more interesting aspects of football for a freshman then was how you found out if you were doing well in the eyes of the coaches. A key player in solving this mystery was equipment manager Henry Hatch.

"The only way you found out that you were doing all right," Rentschler says, "is if Hank Hatch gave you equipment that fit! If you weren't doing as well as they thought you should be doing, Henry wouldn't give you anything that fit. I can

remember vividly that Henry gave Lou Baldacci, our star freshman quarterback, a plastic headgear. The rest of us had to wear
the old leather helmets, but Baldacci got a new one."

Freshmen also never played in games. They just practiced
every day and worked hard. It was late in the year when freshmen practice was scheduled to close that a few of the first-year
players got their real assessment.

"The biggest thing that happened to you as a freshman that
indicated you were doing all right," Rentschler recalls, "was at
the very end of the year before the Ohio State game, the varsity
coaches would keep some of the freshmen back. They released
all of the freshman class except maybe a team of us. Those of us
who they kept ran Ohio State plays against the varsity the week
of the big game. I remember I played Ohio State's Bobby
Watkins all week. By being kept back for that week, it encour-
aged all of us to come back the next year."

It was not an easy life as a freshman Wolverine back then,
but those days are treasured. And although it was a different
time, the experiences of Rentschler and his teammates are
echoed by Michigan men who played before and after them. For
Rentschler and his classmates, it was a group of men working
with the freshmen football team that embodied the spirit of
Michigan.

"Wally Webber was just great with us," Rentschler reflects.
"If we had to miss practice for one reason or another, Wally
would tell us not to worry, because our grades were more important than football."

That should *never* happen

Most coaches will tell you that the pregame speech is
probably a little overrated. The idea of the fired-up
pregame speech that sends a team on to superhuman feats could
be a product of the movies. I mean when Pat O'Brien as Knute
Rockne told his boys to go out there and win one for the gipper,
the pregame speech was immortalized. The reality, though, is
that Ronald Reagan was not George Gipp, and one of your great

All-Americans doesn't come down with a fatal disease every week. It just doesn't work.

As a matter of fact, Bo Schembechler said many times that the upset in college football does not come from the mind of the underdog; rather, the upset is a product of the attitude of the favorite. Coach Schembechler always felt that if you depended on a pregame speech to get your team ready on game day, then you hadn't done a good enough job during the week in practice.

For example, in 1954 the Wolverines were entertaining the Indiana Hoosiers at Michigan Stadium.

"They had a wonderful athlete who played for them named Milt Campbell," Dave Rentschler recalls. "Campbell was best known for winning the gold medal at the Olympics in the decathlon. He was a marvelous athlete and a terrific person. Anyway, he caught a pass late in that game and scored a touchdown, and they beat us 13-9, and they never should have. They should have never beaten us."

That loss stuck in the minds of all the Wolverine players as Indiana came to Ann Arbor the following season. Rentschler was a junior at this point in his career, and he remembers the morning of the game distinctly.

"We had spent the night upstairs at the golf clubhouse," Rentschler says, "and the next morning we'd come down, they'd feed us, and then Bennie [Oosterbaan] would give us a talk. The one talk he gave us that I will never, ever forget is the talk before that particular Indiana game.

"He said to us, 'We lost to Indiana last year, and that should *never* happen! That's a heterogeneous bunch playing for no common cause, and you guys are playing for Michigan! With the fact that you are playing for Michigan, Indiana should *never* beat you.'

"He called them a *heterogeneous* bunch with no common cause," Rentschler laughs.

I'm not sure that approach would have worked on me, because I would have had to go look up *heterogenous* before I would have gotten it, but it sure worked on that 1955 team. They went across the street to Michigan Stadium that Saturday and mauled the Hoosiers 30-0.

By the way, according to *Webster's*: "heterogeneous—of a different kind or nature; unlike or dissimilar in kind; opposed to homogeneous."

Oosterbaan suggested the change

The first Heisman Trophy winner who played for Michigan was Tom Harmon, but when Harmon arrived at Michigan from Gary, Indiana, he was not a primary ball carrier; he was a wingback. In those days, a wingback was more of a pass receiver.

Can you imagine No. 98 not the featured back? Had it not been for a very perceptive assistant coach named Bennie Oosterbaan, football history at Michigan might not be what it is today.

According to lifelong Ann Arbor resident Howard Wikel, it was a change in positions that launched Harmon's legendary career.

"A guy by the name of Paul Kromer was the tailback; Harmon was originally outside as a receiver," Wikel remembers. "It was Oosterbaan who suggested the change to Crisler. Bennie thought Harmon would be better at the tailback and Kromer should move to the wing in the single-wing offense.

"Now remember Kromer was a great, great football player. Ultimately he became a great wingback. It was Ben [Oosterbaan] who probably made the move to benefit both of their careers. Kromer still has to be in the record books some-where."

Kromer is there. In 1938 he led the team in pass receiving and scoring, and in 1938 and 1939 Kromer led the team in punting. Kromer actually was the punter ahead of Harmon in their sophomore and junior years. Harmon, though, was clearly the major player in Maize and Blue in those years. No. 98 led the Wolverines in passing, rushing, and total offense his three varsity seasons. He was the leading scorer in his junior and senior years. Coach Oosterbaan got him in the right spot, and then Harmon did the rest.

According to Wikel, Harmon was a man among boys in those magical years he roamed Michigan Stadium.

"He was the best I've every seen," Wikel says without hesitation. "He was just an outstanding athlete. He played basketball, he ran track, and he was fast! He was big, too. At that time, he was about 198 pounds, he stood about six foot one, and in those days, that was a huge back. There weren't any really big backs. There was *no one* that had the size or the speed like Harmon. He had great cutting ability, and he had great vision."

It was that very ability in Harmon, according to Wikel, that prompted Fritz Crisler to create a new and innovative piece of equipment for his star runner.

"Those days when Harmon was making so many guys miss," Wikel recalls, "was the origination of the tear-away jersey. So many guys would just grab at Harmon. They couldn't catch him, but they grabbed his jersey. So Fritz got the idea for a tear-away jersey, and he gave it to Harmon."

The rest, as they say, is history.

He was a class act

One of the great names in Michigan football history that sometimes gets lost is Harry Kipke. Here was a guy who as a player was as good as they come. In his three years as a varsity player, he played in only one losing game and two ties. In his senior year, he was the captain of a national championship team and an All-America halfback. There is plenty more, too. Kipke is enshrined in the College Football Hall of Fame. He is enshrined in the National Football Foundation Hall of Fame. He is in the Citizens Savings College Football Hall of Fame. He is in the Michigan Sports Hall of Fame and was the only former Wolverine voted as the Walter Camp Man of the Year.

As the Michigan coach in his first five years, Kipke won four Big Ten titles and two national championships. His teams lost just one game and tied three between 1930 and 1933. During the 1929, 1930, and 1931 seasons with Kipke at the helm, Michigan played doubleheaders to generate extra revenue. In these doubleheaders, Kipke's teams outscored their opponents 156-6. He was an affable guy, too. Once, he told the *Saturday Evening Post* that his system of football was "punt, pass and a prayer." Kipke also coined the phrase, "a great defense is a great offense."

Now why do you think I would suggest that he sometimes gets lost in Michigan football history? Well because he came in as a player during the years Yost was the coach, and Yost was clearly the big story. Kipke then coached Michigan just before Fritz Crisler and Tom Harmon showed up in Ann Arbor. Kipke was the bridge between the Yost and Crisler eras. Between those two giants, Kipke was a remarkable success, but he doesn't seem to get the sparkle of Yost and Crisler.

As a player, Kipke was remarkable.

"He was a triple threat," remembers Howard Wikel who knew Kipke well and watched him play, "and he was a fantastic punter. We've lost track of punting out of bounds, but in his day, 'Kip' could always put the ball out of bounds between the 10-yard line and goal line every time."

In an article about Kipke from the time, it was said that he *perfected* the art of punting the ball out of bounds. He won nine letters at Michigan as he was also a standout in basketball and baseball. After graduation, he moved into coaching and actually coached one year at Michigan State before returning to his alma mater.

"Kip had great teams at Michigan in the early 1930s," Wikel remembers, "then he ran on some bad times."

Indeed he did. After his second national title and unbeaten season in 1933, Kipke did not win more than four games a year the next four seasons. In two of those years, Michigan only won one game each season. Kipke was let go as coach after the 1937 season. But although the times were hard, according to Wikel Kipke never stopped working at bringing Michigan back. Wikel even tells us that Kipke became the architect of the Wolverines' glory years even after he was fired.

"Remember this," Wikel says with emphasis, "Kipke had recruited Harmon, Evashevski, Kromer, Westfall, Ingalls, etc. And when he was let go, every one of those great players, to a

Harry Kipke was a legendary player, a superb coach, and a class act.

man, went to Kipke and asked if they should stay at Michigan or go elsewhere. They all had the idea to leave Michigan because Michigan had let Kipke go. Kipke told every one of them, 'No.' He told them all to stay and play for Michigan.

"So Fritz [Crisler] was handed almost an all-world team in 1938. With what they had coming in, Michigan was going to win some football games, and despite that Kipke was let go. There were some hard feelings around but never from Kip. He was a great guy. He was a class act all the way!"

He was such a class guy, in fact, and such a talented guy, that Kipke later served as a regent for the University of Michigan and was the president of the Coca Cola Company. Sounds like a giant to me.

The visionary

O ne of the great aspects of the relationship Fielding Yost and Howard Wikel, a young boy who sat with Yost in his father's drugstore, had was that Wikel as a 13-year-old was not a contemporary of Yost. Wikel became Yost's companion who would listen and not interpret, and Yost's dreams and plans for Michigan could be openly discussed without the doubts or cynicism of an adult mind cluttering the discussion. The best times for this kind of activity came when Yost and young Wikel would pack up their golf clubs and head to the university's new golf course that Yost had just gotten completed with the help of world-renowned Scottish designer, Dr. Alistair MacKenzie.

"The reason I liked to play with Mr. Yost," Wikel remembers fondly, "was that he always took a caddie, and he always hit two balls! So as you played along with him, you could hit two balls also. Since I was getting ready to go to high school and play on the golf team, I loved the practice. The people behind us used to get upset sometimes until, of course, they found out who it was.

"I had the pleasure of playing with him during the mid-1930s, maybe two or three times a week. He didn't play badly. He kind of bumped it along. It was a great experience for me. But the amazing thing is that as we played, we would talk and he would discuss with me his plans for what he called his *university campus*."

Yost's university campus was the vision of what we would call today the *athletic complex* at most universities. The nation's first intramural sports building and the nation's first multipurpose field house were built under Yost's direction. The two buildings still stand today and are still being utilized as vital parts of Michigan's active athletic facilities. As a matter of fact, Yost Ice Arena, the converted field house, is home to Michigan's national powerhouse hockey team coached by Red Berenson.

A world-class golf course, the IM Building, the Field House, and Michigan Stadium, all built in the late 1920s and early 1930s, are all still in use. It is unbelievable to imagine the crystal ball Yost gazed into to create this complex.

The Stadium itself is a monumental visionary achievement. When Yost built it in 1927, the cost was $950,000. There were 70 rows of seats, and capacity was established at 72,000. Wooden bleachers were added above the last row of seats to bring the capacity to 84,401, and in October 1927 a crowd of 84,401 saw a game played between Ohio State and Michigan.

At the time, the capacity was considered way too high. The critics were all over Yost and his vision. They said a college football game would never generate enough interest that would require the size of stadium Yost had built. Putting in the extra foundation to allow for a future second deck was a waste of money according to the critics, but Yost was supremely confident. So much so that he confided in his teenage golfing partner one day on the golf course.

"Mr. Yost was talking about his plans, and even though the Stadium was already built," Wikel recalls the conversation, "he told me that someday, there will be 130,000 people watching Michigan football!

"When he said stuff like that, I used to wonder if the cigar he was chewing on had gotten the better of him! At the time, the Stadium only had a capacity of just over 70,000. To say that it was going to be more than half again, almost double that capacity, you just wondered whether he was off his rocker.

"But clearly he wasn't. He had great foresight. He had great imagination, and he obviously was smart as hell."

Visiting with the greats

The time capsule of Howard Wikel's life coincides with such an amazing cast of characters—Fielding Yost, Harry Kipke, Fritz Crisler, Bennie Oosterbaan, Tom Harmon. All of the Michigan legends, at one time or another, were flesh and blood to Wikel, not just memories or names in a history book.

"The one thing I feel so strongly about is how fortunate I've been all my life to be close to Michigan," Wikel confesses. "And I come right down to today. I consider Lloyd [Carr, Michigan's current head football coach] to be a very close friend, as I did Bo [Schembechler]. I didn't know Bo when [Don] Canham hired him. I thought, 'Schembechler? That's sounds like a disease.' But he and I have become great friends.

"I mean, can you imagine anyone more fortunate than me? I just can't tell you how fortunate I feel to have been close to these people. It's a one-of-a-kind life. There is no one else that I can think of who is still around who has had the opportunity to be close to Michigan for 75 years."

It's not just you who are fortunate; we are fortunate, too. We've had the opportunity to experience these Michigan legends thanks to you!

Celebrate the Variety of Michigan and American Sports in These Other New Releases from Sports Publishing!

Michigan: Where Have You Gone?
by Jim Cnockaert

- 6 x 9 hardcover
- 250 pages
- photos throughout
- $19.95 (2004 release)

Riding with the Blue Moth
by Bill Hancock

- 6 x 9 hardcover
- 256 pages
- photos throughout
- $24.95

Tales from Michigan Stadium
by Jim Brandstatter

- 5.5 x 8.25 softcover
- 200 pages
- photos throughout
- $14.95 (2005 release)

Mike Ditka: Reflections on the 1985 Bears
by Mike Ditka with Rick Telander

- 5.5 x 8.25 hardcover
- 200 pages
- photos throughout
- $19.95

Charlie Sanders's Tales from the Detroit Lions
by Charlie Sanders with Larry Paladino

- 5.5 x 8.25 hardcover
- 192 pages
- photos throughout
- $19.95

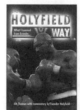

The Holyfield Way: What I Learned from Evander
by Jim Thomas with commentary by Evander Holyfield

- 6 x 9 hardcover • 256 pages
- eight-page photo insert
- $24.95

Detroit Pistons: Champions at Work
by The Detroit News

- 8.5 x 11 hard/softcover
- 128 pages • color photos
- $19.95 (hardcover)
- $14.95 (trade paper)

Dick Enberg: Oh My!
by Dick Enberg with Jim Perry

- 6 x 9 hardcover • 256 pages
- 16-page color-photo section
- $24.95
- Bonus "Beyond the Book" DVD included!

Tales of the Magical Spartans
by Tim Staudt and Fred Stabley Jr.

- 5.5 x 8.25 hardcover
- 200 pages
- photos throughout
- $19.95 (2003 release)

Ferdie Pacheco: Blood in My Coffee
by Ferdie Pacheco

- 6 x 9 hardcover
- 256 pages
- photo insert
- $24.95

All books are available in bookstores everywhere!
Order 24-hours-a-day by calling toll-free **1-877-424-BOOK (2665)**.
Also order online at **www.SportsPublishingLLC.com.**